The Lightning Flash

Translation Happens
Edited by Michèle Cooke

Volume 1

PETER LANG
Frankfurt am Main · Berlin · Bern · Bruxelles · NewYork · Oxford · Wien

Michèle Cooke

The Lightning Flash

Language, longing and the facts of life

PETER LANG
Internationaler Verlag der Wissenschaften

Bibliographic Information published by the Deutsche Nationalbibliothek
The Deutsche Nationalbibliothek lists this publication in the Deutsche Nationalbibliografie; detailed bibliographic data is available in the internet at http://dnb.d-nb.de.

Cover Design:
© Olaf Gloeckler, Atelier Platen, Friedberg

ISSN 1868-7954
ISBN 978-3-631-59714-9
© Peter Lang GmbH
Internationaler Verlag der Wissenschaften
Frankfurt am Main 2011
All rights reserved.

All parts of this publication are protected by copyright. Any utilisation outside the strict limits of the copyright law, without the permission of the publisher, is forbidden and liable to prosecution. This applies in particular to reproductions, translations, microfilming, and storage and processing in electronic retrieval systems.

www.peterlang.de

For my mother

**For things do not seem the same
to those who love
and those who hate.**

Aristotle, *The Art of Rhetoric*

Foreword

Science for real people. I had thought that this would be a good title for a new series: Books that people outside the ivory tower could understand. Written for people who didn't speak the language of academia. But then I realised that such a title would be misleading – and ungenerous. Scientists are real people too. We just usually do our best to hide it.

The world of science is perforce an artificial one. Even in the humanities we are required to show that the individual cases we observe are always and universally true, that they happen in the same way again and again and again. Which is all well and good. But it means we have to leave out the messy bits, the bits that make each thing special, and worthy of our observation. We create a world sterilised of singularity. We've all learnt to feel at home in our own corner of this world, because we've put on the sci-vision glasses and learnt the requisite sci-speak.

Yet, once we leave our own little corner, we tend to feel like non-scientists do: in a strange realm, where people talk in strange tongues about things beyond our ken. It all seems so far away, so detached from the reality that is familiar to us.

But: Isn't it artists – painters and poets – who are supposed to create the fictional worlds? The ones where 'any resemblance to real-life events or persons is purely coincidental'? That's not what scientists do, is it?

Not quite. But: We use words that are foreign to people outside our own specialist field. We write long complicated sentences to make sure we

Foreword

get every argument and counter-argument in, so that no-one can accuse us of having left a single relevant thought un-thunk. We rid our language of all taint of emotionality, to avoid the cardinal sin of subjectivity, and to prove that what we say is true. Yes, we're taught to discard all the features of language that make it real and alive.

This series, *Translation Happens*, arose out of the need to show that we don't have to do this. I believe we can translate our foreign, academic languages into real living ones. This means writing differently, putting things in a different way, but *saying the same thing* – more or less.

And this volume, the first in the series, is a translation: a composition of insights into language, communication and translating. It is one personal interpretation, one particular arrangement of what I take to be the facts. There are, of course, other possible arrangements. We can do the same thing in many different ways: Glenn Gould plays Mozart in a different way from Friedrich Gulda. Same stuff, different rhythm. Translation happens.

Vienna, April 2011

Michèle Cooke
Series Editor

Contents

Foreword	9
Prelude	13
Impromptus	17
No. 1	19
No. 2	23
No. 3	27
No. 4	29
No. 5	33
No. 6	35
No. 7	39
No. 8	43
No. 9	47
Variations	51
No. 1	53
No. 2	59
No. 3	65
No. 4	71
No. 5	83
No. 6	91
No. 7	97
No. 8	103
No. 9	105
Finale	107
Encore I	109
Encore II	109
Thank you	111
Back-up notes	113
Emotional evidence	139
Scientific evidence	141
Index	152

Prelude

Kids – don'tcha love 'em?
Once upon a time, there was a little girl. Her name was Anna. And Anna sometimes had a nasty feeling in her tummy. *Poor darling, is it the tummy-ache again?* her mummy would say. Or: *Anna can't come out to play, she's got tummy-ache.* This made Anna feel almost as bad as the thing in her tummy. *Tummy-ache? Tummy-ache?* Mummy and Daddy never seemed to have it. None of her friends ever had it. What was it about her?

One day, she had to go to the doctor's with her tummy-ache. She sat there, shy and a little embarrassed: Mummy was going to talk about it in front of other people. Her special thing. Then a little boy came in with his mummy. *Well, and what brings you here today? – Poor little Paul's been having a nasty tummy-ache, haven't you, lovey?* At last! Someone like her! This must be luuuv...

*****

What does heaven look like? Not everyone wants to get there. Not everyone believes in it. Some of us may hold up our hands in horror at the thought of all that harp-playing, goody-goodies sitting around eating manna and smiling down benignly on the foolish mortals below. We might reckon our chances of getting there are so slim that it's hardly worth thinking about. Yet, somehow, the word heaven still has a pretty good ring to it. *Heavenly. Seventh heaven. Heaven-sent.* It all sounds rather nice. Feels good.

Prelude

In 2003 the American novelist, Mitch Albom, wrote a book about a man who went to heaven. Eddie was just a regular kind of guy, not particularly smart, not particularly brave, or good, or particularly anything at all. Certainly not angelic. He just did his job and lived his life. Then he died. Landed in heaven – so they said. *They* were five people who showed him his life: the pain, the joy, the sorrow. The missed opportunities, the long years of toil and frustration. Things he was ashamed of, afraid of, or which had hurt him. They also showed him moments of happiness: when he fell in love, when he danced with his wife, or sat under the stars. Eddie was made to see it all.

The five people that Eddie meets in heaven force him to re-live some of the best and worst times of his life. Not too heavenly, one might think. Who wants to go through all that again? Eddie isn't too happy about it either: This is *heaven*? But there's no getting out of it. Heaven is the last stop. They force him to take a good, hard look at the dreams and fears and deeds that constituted his life. Each person, in turn, takes him to a different place in his life, and shows him different things. At first, Eddie is confused, irritated, or just downright angry. No, he doesn't want to look. Why should he? But he has no choice. If he doesn't look, he can't move on to the next person – and he realises fairly soon that that's the only way forward – to move on to the next person and see what they've got in store. Once he's been through all five, he'll have 'made it', will be able to rest in peace. So he has to look at what they show him.

And, every time he looks, things become a little clearer. He begins to understand why they're putting him through this, he begins to see, and he begins to see why. Why he was so angry with his father, why he

Prelude

couldn't fulfil his ambitions. Why he was a coward in the war. Little by little, the mosaic of his memory falls into place, forms a pattern. The pieces start fitting together.

The five people Eddie meets in heaven help him find answers to the questions he didn't know he was asking – and that, in so many ways, made his life a hell. Why? Why? Why? As long as he didn't understand, as long as he didn't get the picture, he would not really be in heaven. Seeing the whole picture was the final test.

*****

I should have died when I was five years old. It was the year I lost my innocence. The year I began to understand that I didn't understand.

Five little girls, in blue pleated skirts and white knee socks. Playtime at primary school, rain falling hard on the roof of the bicycle shed. Our secret meeting place, where we sucked sherbet lemons and whispered silly jokes. Eileen Harris, a bumptious child with greasy pigtails and beady eyes, wanted to tell us where babies came from – she knew. But we all wrinkled our noses: Ugh. Dirty. *Eileen is dirty! Eileen needs a wash! When's your bath-night, Eileen?* Smirks, sniggers, giggles.

- Yesterday.
- I've already had mine.
- Bet you haven't.
- When's yours, then?
- Friday.
- Sunday.
- Yeah, Sunday, to get ready for school.

Prelude

It was my turn next. What on earth should I say? So I just blurted it out: *We don't have bath-night, at our house.*

Silence. Furtive glances. The little English girls smiled at each other. Too polite to say anything. The bell rang. End of play-time.

Why didn't we have a bath-night? All the girls at school had one. It wasn't fair; I needed one too. But how could I tell my Mum, how ask for one, when I didn't even know what it was? That evening, as every evening, we had our tea, helped Mum wash the dishes, played in the garden, watched TV. My little brothers had the bathroom first, because they went to bed before us. Then me and my sister. Filled the bath, made mountains with soap bubbles, splashed, fought and dropped into bed, warm and tired. As we did every night.

*****

I didn't die. I became a translator. Working hard to try to get the picture, to get what people mean. You have to. You have no choice. If you don't, you don't get paid. Somehow, you have to try to understand.

What I've written in this book are some of my attempts at understanding. Or, if you like, why we all want the next guy to have tummy-ache. Or: How I learned to live without a bath-night.

Impromptu (music; plural: *impromptus*)

A short piece of instrumental music that is reminiscent of an improvisation. This means that these works exhibit a certain character of spontaneity. The music shifts from one idea to another without any necessary calculation or caution. These properties give rise to a certain air of carefree latitude …

Impromptus: No. 1

I couldn't tell you quite when it started, but somehow I always knew that I wasn't really English: I was French. Perhaps it was my name, Michele (not a common occurrence in North London in the 1950s), that made me feel a certain *cachet*, that I should really be growing up in the precincts of the Eiffel Tower, not just down the road from Ally Pally (aka Alexandra Palace). Perhaps it was films like *Gigi* and *An American in Paris*, with those chic young girls and men who fulfilled their heart's desires. *Qui sait?* Whatever the case, there was no soupçon of a doubt in my mind that, by the age of nineteen, I would speak fluent French and have transformed myself into a long-legged Parisienne who bought pearls from the Place Vendôme and wore little black numbers from Balmain.

My first French lesson, at the age of ten, was a somewhat sobering experience. Mamzelle (née Miss Mason) had nothing of the Parisienne about her. She was a spare grey Englishwoman who wore brogues and buttoned-up cardigans, and pressed her lips into her face. Except, of course, when she opened them to speak. Then out trickled pretty little phrases like the melodies of a hurdy-gurdy machine. Ready-made, repetitive, but music to my untaught ears. French! Français! A whole new world...

It began with a flickering film of stickmen who kept wanting to buy stamps, even though the stickwoman at the shop insisted she didn't have any. We got that much, because the men waved unstamped envelopes at the woman, and she always shook her head and pointed somewhere else. Mamzelle made us repeat what they said, again and again and again. The only variation, after a few weeks, was that the men began to buy bread, and it was the lady at the baker's who didn't have any (bizarre, *non?*). I refused to admit that I was bored, and got out of it what I could. Copied Mamzelle's intonation, the shake of the head, the funny shapes she made with her lips, the whole French bit. Mamzelle was delighted and made me recite in front of the class when the other children refused to cooperate. I felt for them. Because, just like them, I had absolutely no idea what I was saying. *Shenonnypa. Non, shenonnypa.* I remembered it, because it was my best friend's name: *Jennifer.* Said *à la française*, it was just what the lady at the post-office, baker's, grocery shop was saying: *shenonnyfa*, and what's the difference between a *p* and an *f* if you throw it in with the requisite panache? My affinity for French was confirmed: It came 'naturally', I was destined for Paris and pearls after all.

It wasn't until grammar school, where they teach you (or did in those dark ages) pronouns, adverbs and first person singular, that I realised it wasn't just one word but five (or four?): *Je n'en ai pas*. In other words, *I have not of them*, or as we would say: *I haven't got any*. Did it matter?

At the age of ten, my determination to 'be French' made me do what *we all do* naturally: It made me make the right noises. I did not say words, I had no idea that 'they' were words. I was just making noise that sounded right, and got the desired response. I didn't care about the words because, in my ignorance and naivety, I wasn't even aware of them. I was indeed doing what comes naturally: None of us start by learning *words*; we learn to make noises that can mean things.

Impromptus: No. 1

The French noises I made meant something to my French teacher because she could make sense of them. I certainly didn't. Or rather, the only sense I could make of them was all tied up with my own personal history: wanting to be French, to sound chic, to live in Paris. I had little idea of what I was saying, only some vague notion that it had to do with not having any stamps, or bread, or cheese. Mamzelle, on the other hand, knew very well what I was saying. She actually heard me saying *je n'en ai pas*. She knew nothing of my French friend Shenonnifa, nor that cheese and stamps and bread were all jumbled up in my mind with stickmen and women vehemently shaking their heads at them. She and I came from very different places, yet somehow our paths crossed with the utterance of that noise *shenonnypa*, and she understood me. Or, at least, she knew what I was saying; knew it, in fact, better than I did.

Words don't exist. They are little bits of noise that are, sometimes, separated by bits of silence, or by spaces between them, like the words you are reading now. We all know that all foreigners speak quickly, too quickly. So quickly, in fact, that you can't tell what they're 'really saying', where one word stops and the next one starts. They can't all be suffering from the *shenonnypa* syndrome. Can they? Are we? *Hihowyaduin? Nowaddimean? Gimmeabrake!* People understand us, because they already know what we mean – more or less. Is that enough?

Impromptus: No. 2

> And the whole earth was of one language, and of one speech. And it came to pass, as they journeyed from the east, that they found a plain in the land of Shinar; and they dwelt there. [...]
> And they said, Go to, let us build us a city and a tower, whose top may reach unto heaven; and let us make us a name, lest we be scattered abroad upon the face of the whole earth.
> And the Lord came down to see the city and the tower which the children of men builded.
> And the Lord said, Behold, the people is one, and they have all one language; and this they begin to do: And now nothing will be restrained from them, which they have imagined to do.
> Go to, let us go down, and there confound their language, that they may not understand one another's speech.
> So the Lord scattered them abroad from thence upon the face of all the earth ...

Is this true? It must be, it's in the Bible – Genesis, chapter 11, verses 1-9. There, in black and white. The Word of God. We have evidence to prove it: There really was a Tower of Babel, discovered by the archaeologist Robert Koldewey in 1913. It was 91.48 metres long, 91.66 metres wide, 91 metres high, built to seven or eight levels.

But is it really true? OK, the confusion of tongues – maybe there's some truth in that: We don't all understand each other. There are lots of different languages. But what do we really know about it?

*****

In 1880, Edouard Manet painted a bundle of asparagus. Just a bunch of vegetable stalks, tied up with a bit of string. Not, one would imagine, a motif to inspire great passion or send us into raptures of aesthetic ardour. And yet, the first time I saw this painting, my eyes filled with

Impromptus: No. 2

tears. It moved me beyond words. Was it the simple humility of those bare, bumpy stalks, unadorned, unembellished by any pretension to beauty? Was it the intimation of dirt still clinging to the white stalks, conjuring up the smell of tender shoots and the feel of spring? Perhaps something in me remembered a train-ride through the plains of Austria, a hot, close carriage filled with women in rough clothes and heavy boots, fingers stained with black. Asparagus-pickers, from across the border. Come to earn a pittance for six weeks of back-breaking work. The air was thick with sunlight and the ooze of asparagus juice. The women laughed, ate black bread and bright red peppers, made fun of each other. And there I sat. And knew that in a few weeks I would be sitting in an elegant Vienna restaurant, paying what they earned in a week for a few pretty spears and a blob of sauce hollandaise.

It was probably a mixture of all these things, and much more besides, that brought the tears to my eyes. I have never, to my knowledge, cried when I've seen asparagus at the supermarket, held together with a rubber band and a bit of green plastic. It somehow feels different.

Strange, isn't it, that a picture can make us feel more than the real thing? OK, we can buy the asparagus at the supermarket, take it home, cook it, put butter on it, and eat it. Even if we had enough money to buy Manet's asparagus, we couldn't eat it, because it's not real. All we could do is look at it. And feel it. The feelings are certainly real – my eyes really were wet with tears. The catch in my breath was real. Other people saw the tears too, heard me gasp, so they *must* have been real.

Manet painted a picture that touches us. He shows us a tiny bit of real life, very mundane, very prosaic, yet very moving. He doesn't give us a real-life replica of the asparagus on the supermarket shelves. In fact, he changes things quite a bit. The bluish-purple hue which brings out the whiteness of the stalks, for example, is 'actually' red. Manet used different layers of colour to make us see white asparagus as we would 'really' perceive it. The stipples of colour, of light and shade, fall in the way that he, the painter, chooses, and not in the way that Nature dictates. Manet has put together what is really there – in his own way. What, then, is the real thing?

Impromptus: No. 3

Last summer I bumped into a butterfly. It was light blue with, I think, dark blue and gold patterns on its wings. I'd never seen a blue butterfly before. It fluttered onto my nose and played around my eyes and cheeks and chin for a while. It sat down on a flower and let me come quite close and watch it. Then it flew off, and I lost it in the blue summer sky.

That year, I kept seeing butterflies. They seemed to be everywhere. Was it the unusually sunny weather? Was it because there always are lots of butterflies in that part of Ireland? I didn't see the blue butterfly again, but it was as if he had unleashed a whole summerful of butterflies. Once I'd seen the blue butterfly, I knew that, any day, I could bump into one just like him. They were there, hidden against the sky, I just hadn't noticed them before. Not until one of them flew out at me.

Impromptus: No. 4

How can you write an opera where the leading lady has lost her voice? Antonín Dvořák did it. He composed a work of music for words in which the central figure spends long lengths of time saying absolutely nothing. Dvořák's opera, *Rusalka*, tells the story of a water-spirit who falls in love with a Prince. Her passion is so strong that she is willing to take on mortal form just to be able to hold him in her arms and show him her love. Yet she not only pays the price of her immortality; she's also condemned to a life without words – she loses the gift of speech. She does indeed have to show her love, for she cannot speak it. And such is the folly of woman that she takes all this upon herself.

In opera, of course, to 'speak' is to sing. Words and music are so entwined that they sound as one. Rusalka isn't allowed to sing, but still has to tell her story, express her love, her woe, her torment. She still has to be on stage, and not just stand around twiddling her thumbs. And silence is part of her story.

Dvořák makes silence speak through the noise it makes – through the passions at play in his music. Much of Rusalka's inner turmoil, the tender and the desperate, is rendered through the voice of the harp, both poignant and ethereal. The singer's presence on the stage, the swaying of her body, the gentle and tormented fall of her arms are not what moves us. Without the music, it would all have the effect of a rather wooden dumb-show. It is in combination with the music that Rusalka's actions convey to us the meanings of love and loss. And even without them, if we close our eyes, it is the music that sways us. The music

Impromptus: No. 4

expresses not only silence. It sounds out the depths and heights of what we have all been through, in one way or another. It reaches into every crevice of emotion, to express the unsayable, ineffable yet all too familiar echoes of our life stories.

Who needs words? Why bother with words at all, if music is the thing wherein our imagination is caught? How often do we actually *listen* to the words in an opera? And actually *understand* them? If we're honest, we sometimes don't even recognise the language it's in (Czech? Russian? French? Italian?). Yet we can still enjoy it, feel the emotions, get carried away by the whole thing. Yes, sometimes it helps to have a quick look at the programme before the curtain goes up, just to get the gist of the story. But that really is all we get: the gist. What really matters is something else. The gist of *Romeo and Juliet* is: Two young things fall in love, their parents don't like it, there's a family quarrel, and they end up killing themselves. But whether Shakespeare, Prokofiev or Gounod – there's a lot more to it.

The words don't matter. They're just there to carry the sound, to complement the real message: what the music is telling us. We don't hear words, we hear song. In other words, sound made by somebody's vocal chords in a rhythm, melody, harmony that are not those of everyday speaking. And it's not just in opera that the words don't matter. English and American pop-songs travel the world – who cares what they're saying? We feel the music. French chansons, rebetiko from Greece, Italian folk-songs – we love them. Move to them, move with them. Who cares about the words?

Impromptus: No. 4

It is the silences that make music, the 'spaces' between the notes, the holding and letting go of the piano keys, the harp strings, of breath through a flute. It is the myriad ways in which sound fades into silence that speak to us.

Would Beethoven's Ninth Symphony sound the same with different words? How many of us who have listened enraptured to Beethoven's *Ode to Joy* recognise the words? *Wollust ward dem Wurm gegeben, und der Cherub steht vor Gott.* What we *do* understand is something other than the words; we understand the passion behind them.

Could we, then, just throw in any old words and trust to the force of music? Yes – and no. As long as the words are concordant with the emotional pulse of the music, we can disregard them, let them go. It is only when they are 'right', when they resonate with what the composer wants to tell us, that they don't matter. It is only then that we resonate with them, without listening to them. It is only when words become silent that they can express what they need not say.

And when they are not silent, but loud, when our attention is called to them, something jars. The first time I heard *Rusalka* was in a bad translation from Czech into German. No, I could not compare it with the original version; I did not need to. The words jumped out at us, outran the music or lagged behind. Their rhythm, their sound, was out of joint. Music and text played against each other. Of course, the music won. But how much more beautiful, how much more poignant would it have been to hear them in concord rather than in discord. How much more would we have heard, if we hadn't been forced to listen to the words?

31

Impromptus: No. 5

A week at the sea-side. Boarding-house with damp toast and kippers for breakfast. Blue-white sky, and air that prickles like champagne bubbles. We bought little lighthouses filled with sand, and pink rock to rot our teeth on the train back to London. Six days away from noisy brothers and sisters, of laughing with my friends, learning about cliffs, and castles, and where the tides come from, from the wonderful Miss Fuller. It didn't rain, not once. There were ham sandwiches and cake for tea, and packed lunches we ate on the beach, or in the bus. Who cared if we got sand in our teeth? We just laughed when the wind whipped the top off our ice-cream cones. Who cares, when you're on holiday?

The ferry back to the mainland had dirty black funnels. The sea was choppy grey and green. Gulls screeched, and small children ran up and down the decks, while mothers sat alert, sipping thick brown tea.

By the time the train pulled into Waterloo, we were all exhausted. Thirty smut-faced children, waiting to see their mummies. The holiday was over. The mummies came. One by one, girls and boys perked back to life, their eyes lit up in recognition, and relief. Their mothers hugged and held them in that terribly English way: So prim and proper, as if they weren't really doing it. As if they'd been caught being naughty. The way they nibbled their biscuits at tea-time: *I shouldn't, really...*

Miss Fuller let me sit on her knee. The other children had all been met. And I was very, very tired. A sudden clutter of steps, a woman hurrying

Impromptus: No. 5

down the stairs. Slim, sleek, in close-cut coat and Audrey Hepburn glasses. The vision of elegance.

Ah, here she is! The woman ran and caught me to her. I hid my face in her coat, and felt the rough wool tickle my nose. *So sorry, I missed the Tube...* Hurried. Harassed. Contrite. – My Mum. I didn't even know there were words I could have said. I just held her hand, and was glad to be home.

Impromptus: No. 6

Tourists, as Jean-Paul Sartre might have said, are other people. William Wordsworth certainly thought so, and wrote a poem about it: *On Seeing some Tourists of the Lakes Pass by Reading; a Practice Very Common.*

> What waste in the labour of chariot and steed!
> For this ye came hither? Is this your delight?
> There are twenty-four letters, and those ye can read;
> But Nature's ten thousand are blanks in your sight.
> Then throw by your books, and the study begin;
> or sleep, and be blameless, and wake at your inn.

How dare tourists come to Wordsworth's beloved lakes and pass them by, oblivious to their beauty and the 'book of Nature'? Are they blind? Have they no feelings? Wordsworth, at least, is convinced of their turpitude.

I know what he means. Except what drives me mad are not people reading books, it's the ones with the digital cameras. I sit on the harbour wall overlooking a little bay in the Irish Sea, feeling rather poetic myself. At one with the Universe, watching gulls crying against the wind, the hush of waves against the shore – that sort of thing – when some tourists of my own suddenly mar the scene. Eye glued to camera. Click. Click. *Stand there* – click. *No, here* – click. Are they senseless? Are they blind? Can't they take the *feel* for the place home with them? Click, click, click. Philistines.

The clicking stops. The man and woman stop, try different angles with the camera. A rainbow arches across the bay, thick, bold, brighter than

Impromptus: No. 6

gold. And then another; two rainbows, one above the other, illuminating sea and sky, the islands in the distance and the hills behind us. It just won't fit into the little electric eye, so they give up. Just stand there, very still, and look. And look, and look. Rain sweeps in from the horizon, onto the esplanade. The couple button up their coats, and run for cover.

Tourists are other people, until they stop acting like tourists. What would Wordsworth have made of it?

> My heart leaps up when I behold
> A rainbow in the sky

His tourists, and 'mine', may not have put it like that. They may have just said: Cool!

Wordsworth was cross (let's call things by their name) because the tourists refused to see what he saw: 'Nature's beauty' was 'blank in their sight'. That's what bothered me, too. My tourists were messing around with my world, trying to shove it into a camera, oblivious to the *real* beauty of the place. It was only when they started seeing it the way I did that I stopped being cross at them. It's alright, they're seeing the beauty I see (or so I supposed).

Did their hearts leap up? Probably – whose wouldn't? Who am I, or who indeed is Wordsworth, to assume they are aesthetically obtuse simply because their take on things is different? They did stand rapt in wonder. Maybe they couldn't find the words; maybe they didn't want to. Maybe they just let out a silent sigh. *Tourists only see what they want to see.* Well, yes...

Impromptus: No. 6

What Wordsworth, and I, and all of us do, is put up a fight for the way we see things, the way we relate to things. *No, look, you have to see it like this. Well, the way I see it...*

It's curious just how annoyed we can get. Wordsworth's attack on his poor unsuspecting tourists is very caustic: There was absolutely no point in their coming to the lakes, it was a waste of time and effort for all concerned. If they're too stupid to understand Nature's book they may as well stay cooped up in their inn and sleep the time away. His words were lofty, certainly. But the sentiments?

Wordsworth is not just attacking; he's defending. We all have a vested interest in maintaining the 'rightness' of how we see, feel, experience things. That is how things *are*. When other people come along and suggest that things might be otherwise, it tends to rock our boat. And we tell them to stop. With poetry, with rude remarks – or restrictive immigration laws.

When things mean something to other people that they don't mean for us, it's the others who are tourists in our world. They barge in, with their lack of appreciation, their inability to understand. Other people are always tourists in our own meanings, in our version of the story. And, like all tourists, there's no getting away from them.

Hell is other people, as Sartre did say, because other people behave like tourists.

*****

Impromptus: No. 6

> I have slept with her so long,
> With my solitude
> She never leaves me,
> My faithful shadow
> She follows everywhere I go
> To the ends of the earth
> ...
> We have made a truce
> And now walk gently hand in hand
> I do not know what this pact will mean
> Do I accept the peace
> Or must I go on fighting?
> ...
> No, she never leaves me,
> My solitude
>
> Georges Moustaki, Ma Solitude

We try to get out of hell, out of being alone with what things mean to us, by trying to get to heaven: We try to make people see things how we see them. We try to make them understand.

But, can it work? Don't you have to die to get to heaven?

Impromptus: No. 7

What sound does a raindrop make? Well, you might say, it depends. Are we talking about a soft summer rain? Cold, mean winter rain? Hot rain in the tropics, or the sweet rain of spring? Quite. Frédéric Chopin thought along those lines too. He was not at all happy when people started referring to his Prelude No. 15 as the Raindrop Prelude. For, after all, what sound do raindrops make?

I had heard Chopin's Prelude No. 15 many times before I learnt that it had a name. I can't say exactly what I felt when I listened to it. Certainly something silvery, ripply, delicate, heart-rending. I first heard its name in English: Raindrop. Ah, yes, of course. It does sound like raindrops: Liquid pearls falling through space. Then I learnt what it was called in German: *Regentropfen*. Mmh. Yes, of course. Green, dripping, fresh. I had a little more trouble with the French: *Goutte d'eau*. Silvery-grey, plump, scintillating. But, yes, why not. I don't know which name came first, which was the 'original'. And I don't care. In fact, there was no original, because Chopin didn't give it a name. It just was.

The names sounded fine to me, even seemed to make what I heard clearer. Oh yes, that's what I'm feeling...

The names rang true, for me. And, of course, for the people who coined them in the first place. But *raindrop* – or, more probably, *goutte d'eau*, did not ring true for Chopin. Raindrops, drops of water, was all that other people heard in his music. For him, it was much more, so much more, that it could not be squeezed into words, let alone one word. The

39

Impromptus: No. 7

amplitude of his thought and feeling was narrowed by the act of naming. Sticking a label on the delicate nuances of expression was like trying to bottle up an ocean breeze. You can't do it.

Funny, what words can do. After I'd read that Chopin rejected the naming operation, I realised that they weren't raindrops after all: Yes, you *can* hear a lot more in it than that... Am I just fickle, easily swayed by what other people say? Maybe. And maybe words – or the lack of them – make us look at things, hear things, feel things, in a certain way. They say that Chopin composed the Prelude No. 15 in a night of storm and wind. What if 'they' had called it the *Thunder Prelude*? One of Chopin's interpreters, Alfred Cortot, called it *Death is waiting in the shadows*. (*Mais la Mort est là, dans l'ombre*). A very different sensation, is it not? There is also some doubt as to whether it was in fact Prelude No. 15 that Chopin composed that night; it might have been No. 6, or No. 8. Are they all raindrops – or none of them?

Giving Chopin's Prelude the name *Raindrop* gives us something to call it. It calls up raindroppy feelings. That's fine. We know what they're like (more or less), have no trouble imagining them, relating to them. We know where we're at.

But Chopin meant more. And was irritated that people didn't get it. It's good to feel that we know where we're at, that we understand what's being told us. When we give things a name, we say *Yes, that's what it is*. We know what it is. We have a handle on it. Not having a handle can be disconcerting. It throws us. If it's not raindrops, what is it then?

Impromptus: No. 7

A friend, eighty-six years old, told me, with tears in her voice, how she had gone to a self-service restaurant with her husband, also eighty-six. He bagged a table, while she went to get the food. Coming back with the tray, she couldn't find him. Until she realised the old man in the checked shirt was the man she'd been loving and seeing every day for the past sixty years. The old man...

Seeing what we know in a different light can be a real shock. An old man, not-raindrops – how do you get a grip on it?

> Yes, I am just like you
> Like any one of you
> You, like grains of sand
> Like blood that is always shed
> And fingers forever crushed
> Believe me, just any one of you
> I longed to do you good
> You, so much a part of me
> But my words scatter lost in the wind
> Fall dumb in depths of silence
> Fade fast in the dim-lit night.
> Deaf to the sound of my soul
> Cold to the touch of my hand
> Blithe-limbed you pass me by
> And heed not my long low cry
>
> After Louis Aragon, *J'entends, j'entends*

Frédéric Chopin, like Louis Aragon, wanted us to hear what he was saying, and not simply tread the usual, well-known paths.

Words help us get a grip. But the grip can sometimes get too tight.

Impromptus: No. 8

I've still got my son's first pair of shoes – and he took his first steps over twenty years ago. Vincent van Gogh painted a pair of shoes that pierce your heart. He shows us the toil and hardship of one person's life in the boils and creases and worn-down soles, in the tired boot-laces and sagging tongues. He shows us in these mundane objects a whole human life. When we look at the painting, a chord reverberates within us. If we have even for a moment looked at the shoes of someone we love – child, parent, friend, lover – and felt their presence in them, we have an inkling of what van Gogh is saying. We've 'been there' too. We re-cognise something in the picture. That's why it says something to us.

Impromptus: No. 8

We don't have to have looked a pair of shoes the way van Gogh did. It is not because we have felt exactly what he felt (how could we?) that we are moved. It is because the shoes he has painted stand for the shoes we have seen in a similar light, the lives of the people we have loved, which have left an imprint on their shoes. To feel that someone else has seen what we have is what moves and comforts us. It's not just me, I'm not alone. It doesn't matter if they're garden wellies, ballet shoes or biker boots. We know that something rings true. *True* doesn't mean exactly the same. *L'exactitude n'est pas la vérité*, as Henri Matisse once said. Exactitude is not the same as truth. The painting speaks to us because it reveals, in one very personal expression, the particular, personal emotions of each one of us. The shoes are not abstract, archetypical shoes. They stand there as witness to one human being's hard-working lot. The minute personal detail of these worn, tired shoes brings out the stark truth of their history. And it is in this nakedness, shorn of any context that can cover, or distract us from this truth that they appeal to us. *Pars pro toto*. Van Gogh's shoes are one expression of what we have all been through. They tell a truth that we can all know.

In Edith Wharton's novel, *The Age of Innocence*, Newland Archer gives up the love of his life to remain loyal to the girl he had promised to marry before he learned the meaning of passion. Towards the end of his life, through an indiscretion on the part of his son, he discovers that his wife had known all along of the sacrifice that he had always held secret.

> It seemed to take an iron band from his heart to know that, after all, someone had guessed, and pitied... And that it should have been his wife moved him indescribably.

Impromptus: No. 8

He had, after all, not been alone. Even though it is only in retrospect that his wife's understanding of his sorrow becomes known to him, he derives comfort from it. He was not alone. Someone else knew. And though her sorrow was not exactly his, they shared a common pain and knew a common secret. Exactitude is not necessarily truth. Archer's wife knew his truth because she was partaking of it.

Anna didn't have the same tummy-ache as little Paul. It's quite probable that their tummies were hurting for very different reasons. But just to know that she wasn't the only one, that someone else had 'that kind of thing' too, made her feel better. She wasn't the only one – she was OK.

One tummy-ache isn't the same as another tummy-ache. But same enough to know what we're talking about. We might call Chopin's Prelude No. 15 *Raindrop*, *Goutte d'eau*, or *Regentropfen*. Not exactly the same thing. But same enough to know what we're talking about. Each 'label' captures a different facet of the overall picture. *Pars pro toto*. That's why Chopin didn't want to label his music. Labels reduce the picture. No word can say it all. No human expression can reveal the whole picture. The words we use, the pictures we paint or the music we write each give us a different focus, a different twist of the kaleidoscope. The picture is always the same but the light always falls differently, and the bits of coloured glass always fall in a different pattern. We cannot hear, or say, the same thing. *Raindrop* is not *Goutte d'eau*, and my son's baby boots are not van Gogh's shoes. But they're same enough. We know what people mean.

Yet, how much is enough? How much can anyone understand?

Impromptus: No. 9

Did I learn to live without a bath-night? Well, no, as you will no doubt be relieved to hear. What I did learn was that I already had one. Or rather, something that other people might regard as one.

When I was five years old (and, *entre nous*, for quite a while after that), I had no idea that other people called things by different names. I thought words meant things: *garden, school, bath*. You said the words, and everyone knew what you meant. We all spoke English, didn't we? The incident in the bicycle shed was the first crack in the picture. I knew the words, but what did they *mean*? There was nothing I could relate them to. It didn't feel good, not knowing what the other little girls meant. I could feel there was something they all knew, and I wasn't part of it. What was it? And why wasn't I part of it?

What they knew was what they saw. The night they had a bath was special, different from all the other nights – they were just a hazy wodge of things. But bath-night stood out. That's why they had a word for it. And that's why I didn't. The obvious things don't stick out; they're just there, and we don't even know it. Yes, of course I knew I had a bath every night, because I did. But it literally wasn't worth mentioning. And you don't need a word for something that's not worth mentioning. My school-friends needed to mention it. That's all. And because I did know, 'really' what they were talking about, because I had the 'same thing, really' I managed to figure out, after a while, what they were getting at. I just didn't know I knew, until something forced me to take a second look. Not just at them – at me. The something was irritation, confusion, and pain. It

47

Impromptus: No. 9

hurt, not to feel part of things. Not to know why they looked at me in that funny way. It hurt, not to understand.

The second look was through their eyes. What was it that made them look at me like that? How would I look at me, if I were them? *Foreigner. Dirty. Doesn't wash.* Maybe. These may be the labels they stuck on me, without even knowing it. Maybe they just thought: *Funny, how can you not have a bath-night?* Perhaps I'm putting too much of my story into theirs. Perhaps not. That's the risk, when you start trying to understand: You might get it wrong. But what's the alternative? If you don't try, you always stand there alone, you don't stand a chance of being part of it.

Looking back, I guess I could have said:

We have lots of bath-nights. You only have one?
Or
Every night is bath-night at our house.
Or simply
Bath-night? Bath-night? We don't have them, at our house.

Coulda, woulda, shoulda.

Maybe I could tell my son, so that he'll know what to do, if ever... But then, you never can tell anyone anything. They have to get it for themselves.

Translators have to 'get it' to make a living. We all do it to live. No-one will ever know exactly what we mean. But same enough is good enough.

Impromptus: No. 9

In fact, it's just great. Feeling that people get you, and that you get them — there's nothing like it. It's almost like heaven.

And, if we don't manage it? What if we can't get it? Well, *c'est la vie*. Thank goodness.

*****

But, what if this is only my version, only *my* way of seeing things. How do I know, after all, that it's not just me? Read on.

Variation (music; plural: *variations*)

The presentation of a thought in new and varied aspects, yet keeping the essential features of the original. In a composition, the varied repetition of a theme.

Variations: No. 1

How do you know a circle is round? The artist Giotto, who lived in Italy from roughly 1266 to 1337, knew the answer. Unlike many other artists, he enjoyed great acclaim in his own day; so much so that the Pope (Benedict IX) sought him out to commission some paintings for Saint Peter's Cathedral in Rome. However, the Pope, being an astute man, didn't want to grant such a prestigious contract to anyone just on hearsay, on the basis of mere reputation. He needed some proof that Giotto really was as good as people said. He sent one of his courtiers to Tuscany

> ... to find out what sort of man Giotto was and what his work was like. On his way to see Giotto and to find out whether there were other masters in Florence who could do skilful work in painting and mosaic, this courtier spoke to many artists in Siena. He took some of their drawings and then went to Florence itself, where one day he arrived at Giotto's workshop to find the artist at work.
> The courtier told Giotto what the Pope had in mind [...] and, finally, he asked Giotto for a drawing which he could send to His Holiness. At this Giotto [...] took a sheet of paper and a brush dipped in red, closed his arm to his side, so as to make a sort of compass of it, and then with a twist of his hand drew such a perfect circle that it was a marvel to see. Then, with a smile, he said to the courtier: 'There's your drawing'. [...] The courtier replied, 'Is this the only drawing I'm to have?'- 'It's more than enough,' answered Giotto. 'Send it along with the others and you'll see whether it's understood or not.
>
> From Giorgio Vasari's *Lives of the Artists*

The courtier wasn't too happy, to have to take the Pope back a simple red circle as proof of the artist's talent. Still, he explained how Giotto had

Variations: No. 1

painted the circle without the aid of a compass, and the Pope (with the help of a few 'knowledgeable courtiers') realised the extent of Giotto's genius. He got the job, and the rest, as they say, is history.

Is it? Today, we're not even sure if this story is true. Vasari, who wrote about the lives of artists from Cimabue to Titian, may have got it wrong, as he did many other biographical details.

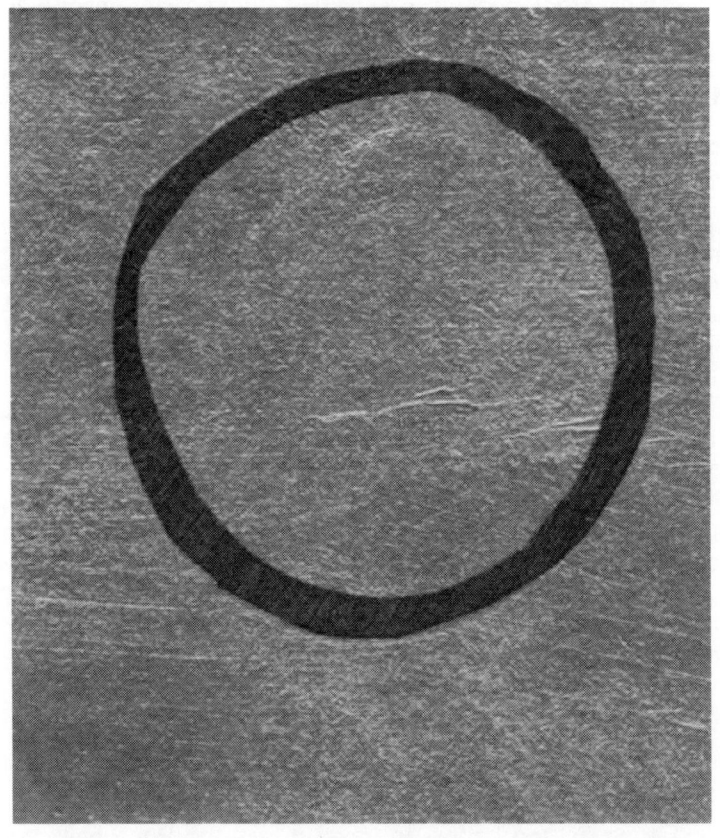

A round circle?

But it certainly sounds good, and also illustrates a point: You don't need exactitude to get things right. Giotto didn't need a compass, or any other scientific equipment. And the Pope didn't need to calculate the area of the circle ($r^2\pi$) or the circumference ($2r\pi$) to recognise its beauty – but he did need a little help from his courtiers. Giotto, the envoy, Pope Benedict, and his advisers, all *knew* that they were looking at a wonderfully round circle.

So, where do exactitude and precision get us? Who needs to know that area = $r^2\pi$? Can't we just look at the thing? Well, yes: We can, and we do. And, very often, that is all we need. But not always. Sometimes we want to know why things that we know are as they are. Why is the sky blue? Why do birds sing? Why do we call the simplicity of Giotto's circle *beauty*? We want to know whether what we know is real.

And, of course: We want to know why we want to know. Yes, OK, there's the fundamental human need to understand. Or our basic urge to make sense of things, to create order in the chaos of the world, to find our way through the labyrinth. Like the Little Prince in St. Exupéry's story, we can go on asking *Why?* forever. The Little Prince never let go of a question once he'd asked it. *How can you own five million stars? If you own five million stars what can you do with them?*

Not only does he never let go of a question; he asks very simple ones. What does it mean to *tame someone? Why do roses have thorns?* Silly, really. Everyone knows why. In his ignorance of the ways of the planet Earth, the Little Prince looks at all its 'obviosity' with the innocence of an outsider. And by asking simple questions about things we all know, he

Variations: No. 1

makes us poor benighted adults look at what is obvious, at what everyone knows, in a new light. His innocent questions light up what we didn't even know was in the dark.

There are lots of Little Princes running around, asking silly-sounding questions about the blatantly obvious, or the seemingly irrelevant. Why do we have grandmothers? Do birds speak in dialects? Or: What does grammar have to do with Hitler?

But unfortunately, we're not called princes or princesses; we're called scientists. At least, we are in German.

Scientists are not just physics nerds, or people who work out the structure of DNA. They are nerds who keep asking *Why?* About anything. About what is obvious to anyone with an ounce of common sense. And that is why: They want to get behind the common, everyday sense of things and see if there is more to it than meets the eye.

Giotto knew his stuff. And he knew that he knew. I wasn't as sure as Giotto. I wanted to find out if what I knew was really true. So I became a scientist.

Because the other thing about scientists is that, like Pope Benedict with Giotto's circle, they need back-up. They need to make sure that other people think what they think: *Is the circle really round? Really OK? Do you think so too?* Yes, everybody likes to feel that; it makes us feel good when other people say, *Hey, that's just what I think.* We feel reassured.

But scientists make a big thing of it. They back up what they say by saying: So-and-so said that too. *Other people have seen what I see.*

Of course, back-up is only back-up. Telling you that Aristotle said something doesn't prove it's right. It simply provides more evidence.

Is it true that there is more to the words we use than meets the eye? Can we show that there really is something there between the lines? Can we say: *I know what you mean* with the same conviction as $E=mc^2$? Is it really true, or just a feeling?

Dr. Johnson famously kicked a stone to prove it was real. He was fed up with all the philosophical debates about Reality. How do we know a stone is really there? Kick it, and you know.

But where do you start? Language, life, feelings – it all hangs together. What's real, what isn't? Where do you start tracing the beginning of a circle? First rule: Start from where you are. So I started with what I knew:
People don't understand each other.
But they sometimes do.
Why not? How? Why?
And this is what I came up with.

Variations: No. 2

Life is like a tea-bag.
Why?
Why not?

Tea-bag

Life: Rebecca, Lilly, Hannah and Molly Cooke

Variations: No. 2

The old Tommy Cooper joke works on a principle we all know: If you can say life is like a tea-bag, you can say anything is like anything else. Pointless: that doesn't get you anywhere. The joke also assumes that we're waiting for a punchline, like in the Eleanor Roosevelt tea-bag joke.

A woman is like a tea-bag.

Why?

You don't know how strong she is until she gets into hot water.

It also works with the element of surprise. We don't expect women to be compared to tea-bags – first surprise. Women and tea-bags are both strong – OK. Then we get the pun on hot water – second surprise. The Tommy Cooper joke takes this a step further. It gives us the surprise of comparing life and tea-bags, and then leaves us up in the air.

Where does the surprise come from? At first glance, we can't see that life and tea-bags have anything in common.

We couldn't say why they are different, either. We wouldn't know where to start because, again we have nothing to go on. Like chalk and cheese, or low-fat cheese and Roquefort. If things have absolutely nothing in common, we can't say why they're alike – or why they're different. Everyone knows that, and every comedian knows that we know.

Once two things have been brought together – Life and the Tea-bag – we start trying to see what there could be between them. Life is like a tea-bag because it ends up soggy; because it's boring until it ends up in hot water; because there's nothing quite like it ... Somehow, however unlikely it may be, we try to find some sort of connection, to relate them.

Variations: No. 2

Again, this is what all the *What's the difference between...?* jokes depend on: We try to make sense of things by seeing connections.

Of course, we all see different connections: you, me, Tommy Cooper, Eleanor Roosevelt. And we can, too, see each other's connections; we can get the joke. In fact, seeing the connection between women and tea-bags (or the non-connection between life and tea-bags) *is* the joke. But, not only do we all see different connections; we all see different things.

This philosophical problem, like many others, is exemplified in an exchange between Pooh Bear and Piglet in *The House at Pooh Corner*. Eeyore, who has inadvertently taken a plunge in the river, is waiting to be rescued. Pooh has the brilliant idea of throwing stones to create waves which will wash Eeyore to the shore. And it works!

The problem arises when Eeyore denies that Pooh has had any Idea at all. He, Eeyore, had got out of his predicament all on his own. (Sound familiar?). Pooh had nothing to do with it. And Pooh, a Bear of Very Little Brain, begins to doubt whether he had had an Idea after all. He finds that things (e.g. Ideas) which seemed like Things to him, weren't always Things once other people started looking at them. (Sounds familiar...) What he took for a Thing – his brilliant Idea – was nothing – No-Thing, to Eeyore. Luckily for Pooh, and for all of us, loyal little Piglet tells him his Idea really was a Thing, and a very good one, too.

Which illustrates the well-known principle that we only see what we want to see. And things that make us feel uncomfortable, like having to be

Variations: No. 2

rescued by a Bear of Very Little Brain, are often things that we don't like to see.

The world isn't full of Things waiting to be seen, or not seen. The world isn't full of any Thing: It just is. Which may be great for the world, but not so great for us, for it means we all have the Pooh Bear problem. How do I know a thing is there if I'm the only person seeing it? Answer: You try to find a 'Piglet', who will tell you they saw it too. You get a back-up.

Human infants don't know where they 'stop' and their mothers, or other care-takers, 'start'. It's all one, to them. They stick their fingers in their mouth when they're hungry, and only when no milk comes out do they begin to cry, because it's not Mummy. They are, literally, at one with their world. Only gradually do they begin to bring the world around them into focus, to distinguish what is important for them and what isn't. Of course, this process kicks in from the moment of birth, when babies take their first breath, the first shock of recognition: This stuff around me is vital for my survival. Infants learn to *place* people and other 'stuff' going on around them in a gradual process of differentiation. Person-who-holds-me, person-who-feeds-me, thing-where-milk-comes-out, wet-stuff-on-my-bottom... Mummy, Daddy, bottle, happy...

What we all learn to do, is indeed to place the bits of the world we notice. We notice them because we need them. We put them into some sort of order. And this order is always in relation to our place, to where we are. A human baby doesn't have to place ultrasonic waves into the order of her life, because it has nothing to do with her. A bat baby, on the other hand, will have to learn to recognise them very quickly, or she will soon be a dead bat baby. The ultrasonic waves are there, but we don't 'need' them (not until we have to do physics at school). So we don't relate to them; they are not Things, for us. We make Things, by seeing how they fit in with us. Things become Things when we place them, put them in order and make sense of them.

We need order if we want to understand anything, if we want to know what sort of Thing it is. We are not the only ones: Nothing can work without order. Lack of order, as we all know, is mess. The world is one great big Order.

So, where does the mess come from? The 'mess' doesn't come from lack of order, but from too much of it. Put on the human scale: You have your order, and I have mine. Pooh Bear had his, and Eeyore had another. Put the two together, and 'mess' happens. Pooh was hurt, Eeyore was cross. I think you're talking rubbish, and you think I'm too stupid to see your point.

What happens here is not that there is no order; there are two different orders clashing against each other. In other words, what the physicists call dis-order. When different orders of Things clash, we get a jumble of orders, not just mess. This is why we can usually sort it out.

We sort it out by using the tea-bag principle: We look for new connections. We re-scramble all the Things and create a new set of order. Why is Life like a tea-bag? When is red really white? Why is a feeling like a stone?

Variations: No. 3

I have an Irish friend called Mary. She reminds me of Chopin: She's not happy about the naming game either. Specifically, she's not happy about her name: Mary. She says it doesn't express who she is. Anyone could be called Mary – and, in her generation, almost everyone is. All the things that the name implies: meek, mild, Catholic, long-suffering, etc. etc., have little to do with who she really is. She says she would rather be called Isolde: elegant, passionate, brave... Being called Mary made people think of her in a certain way, and treat her in a certain way. It was her handle. And, although she knew she wasn't *really* a Mary, somehow she couldn't escape from it. In lots of ways, she became a Mary. 'Ah', she would say, '*if only I'd been called Isolde...*'

My friend Mary, being Mary, and not Chopin, did not rant and rage at the people who named her – her parents. Yes, it was a name that stamped her, but it was also the name that they had chosen. With love. It was a name that they bestowed on their baby girl. It meant something to them. Was it their fault that my friend didn't like what it meant? That she felt it didn't correspond to how she saw herself?

So Mary-who-wasn't-really-Mary accepted her parents' meaning. But she knew (and her friends knew, too) that she could also be an Isolde.

Naming is an act of love. It looks at someone, at something – and sees them. We name what we see. If people don't see anything in us, it bothers us. Chopin was angry that Liszt and others saw only raindrops. But at least they saw (and heard) *something*: Better drops of water than

Variations: No. 3

nothing. What we don't name, we don't see. Or, if we do see it, we pretend it's not there, don't know how to deal with it, can't grasp it.

If Mary's parents hadn't given her a name, what, or who, would she have been? The very idea is monstrous: What sort of parents wouldn't give their child a name? It's against the law. It is also against the law to give your child a name that demeans their dignity and self-worth. The law-givers are only too aware of the shaping power of names. Without a name, Mary would have been nobody, no-one. No-name.

But, of all things, *Mary*. Common or garden *Mary*. Call out Mary in the playground and dozens of little girls will come running. Same thing at college, same thing at work. Mary – the prototypical Irish name. And who likes to be typical – the *type* to be called Mary (or anything else)? We don't even like to be called 'Typical You...' Give someone, something, a name and you make it typical. It represents a type.

What is a *rose*? A type of flower...
What is a *dog*? A kind of animal...
Who is your friend? Mary...
A fifty-year-old...
An Irish woman...

When we give a thing a name, we always make it a kind of something.

We'll call our little girl Mary – it suits her...

Does it? Give someone or something a name and you make something special, unique, one among many, into one of a kind. Everything that has a name is both unique and one of a kind. That's why we have names (words) for things. Mary's parents thought it suited her, because they had an idea of what a Mary is like, and because they saw this (or wanted to see this) in their own special little girl.

Having a name, or a word for something, ties that one particular thing to all the other things that are like it. Having a name for something places it in a certain context, a certain order. If we don't have a word for something, we can't place it. Having a word for something places it in the order of things. It unites the particular with the universal, the one-of-its-kind with the others-of-its-kind.

*****

There was a boy at school called David Goldman. We all adored him. He was eighteen, we were just eleven – and in love. Tall, good-looking, blue eyes, kind, funny, good at sports. You name it, he had it. Of course we were in love.

And of course my brothers and sister found out. And of course they teased me about it. *You love David Goldman! You love David Goldman!* That was bad enough. But then the other kids on the block got in on it. *David Goldman? He's a Jew isn't he? Bet he's a Jew.* I had no idea. He wasn't an anything. He was just David Goldman, in all his splendour.

A Jew. Why did it sound so awful? Because it reduced this wonderful, never-before-seen young man to one single element of all that he was. An element that others chose to single out and label him with. For them he was not an unique constellation of attributes. He was a *Jew*. One of many, with no other distinguishing characteristics. Nothing to make them special or individual. Nothing to show their life histories, their very own personal version of the human story. A *Jew*. Not: *Jewish*. Robbed of all other human characteristics.

It works with almost any word. Take an adjective: blonde, black, foreign and turn it into a 'name': a Blonde, a Black, a Foreigner. It gets worse if you replace the little word 'a' by 'the': the Jew, the Black, the Foreigner. It gets worse because then we turn individual people into archetypes, into beings that are absolutely and nothing but 'typical'. Devoid of any humanising features. And that, as we all know, is exactly what happened, and exactly why the Jew, the Black, the Foreigner, could be treated the way they were. Robbed of all the features that distinguish us as human beings, it becomes so much easier to treat us inhumanly.

When naming leaves out what is individual, it gives the illusion of being universal: the Jew, the archetype of all that is Jewish. But: Nothing that actually is can ever be an archetype, because every thing happens only once, in a one-off constellation of circumstances. When we give typical examples of animals, processes or anything at all, we always leave out the distinguishing features which make it individual, which make it itself, and not something else. Human beings are no exception. None of us has ever been here before or lived the same life before (even if we believe in reincarnation, the life lived is always different). Making people 'universal' means making them non-beings, turning them into objects with no subjective existence.

Variations: No. 3

Der Jude

The Jew

Variations: No. 3

Naming is not always an act of love. It is also an act of tyranny, violence, and annihilation. Putting things into words always means putting them into some sort of box, fixing some sort of label on them. The question is: How much space does the box have? Is there room to breathe – or not?

My friend Mary could have changed her name, if she'd really wanted to. Chopin did not want to give his music names, but other people did it for him. Does that make Mary less of the Isolde she sees herself as? Or Chopin's music less meaningful? When the word boxes leave room to breathe, the things that are put into them can move, expand, turn this way and that. They can get out of the boxes. Mary could see she was also an Isolde, and could live like one. We can choose to hear the Raindrops – or not. Words merely hint at what things could be, and leave space for them to be seen, felt or lived differently.

Words need space. And the biggest space is silence.

Variations: No. 4

Darling Ducks, Jakob Ritt

What's the story? What happens between the first picture and the last one? He sees her, she sees him, they go on a few dates, fall in love. Then the inevitable happens: they quarrel, they make up. Happy ending.

Variations: No. 4

How do we know all this? It all happens in the space between the pictures. The real story is what we don't see.

Without the space, we have no room for imagination. No room to bring in our own thoughts and feelings. Each of us probably tells a slightly different version of the ducks' love story. But we probably all come to more or less the same conclusion. The pictures give us a few clues, and we make up the rest. If there were no space between the pictures, there would be no room for us. There would be no room for us to draw the parts of the story together. The silent space lets us make our own story out of the pictures somebody else has put out there.

What does silence sound like in German? Or Japanese, or Hungarian? The same as in English? The sounds are all spaced differently. The intervals between the words fall with a different frequence. There are different sorts of silence. We all know that.

Silence is never nothing. Space is not empty. Silence is not-saying something. We can only have silence if we know that there are words around it that have been said, could be said, will be said.

Of course, silence is not only created by words. We notice silence by what it is not: When a lawnmower stops droning, when a baby stops crying, when a bird ceases to sing. The silence before a storm, before waves crash to the shore, before the final crescendo. Silence is the anticipation of what is to come, or the memory of what has been. It is never nothing, and never stands alone.

Variations: No. 4

Dvořák let Rusalka, his water-spirit, speak her silence by creating sound. The music told us she could not talk; it was not saying nothing. Neither did Rusalka's silence say nothing: It told of her love, her devotion, and her helplessness. Her lover, the Prince, understood what she was saying – until he let himself be tempted into the coarser medium of the 'concrete evidence' of passion offered him by the other woman. Silence means something.

Music itself is the arrangement of silence. The space between the notes shapes what we hear. And how this space is filled by silence is how the music works.

Language, too, works with silence. Words need space around them to be recognised as words. Otherwise we just have a stream of more or less meaningless sounds.

Shenonnypa. We actually need to know each single word: *Je n'en ai pas* before we can put them together in some meaningful order. We need the space between them so we can join them together.

Of course, space has its problems. Look at the blank computer screen, a picture frame, a fresh blanket of snow. You could put almost anything into it or on it. That's the fascination – and the fear. The first page is always the most difficult to write: all that expanse of possibilities. Where do you start? What if it goes wrong? Once you get started, the words you've already written, the notes you've already heard, the colours and lines you've already painted, begin to show you the way, narrow down the possibilities – and the margin for error.

Variations: No. 4

There are words that take up lots of space, and words that are smaller. Words like *Being* or *Time* are full of space: Where do they start? Where do they end? Something like *I am* or *Yesterday*, on the other hand, is a lot tighter, and a lot more precise. The margin for error is much smaller. There's only one person who can say *I am* and that's always *me*. *Yesterday* is always the day before today, but *Time* and *Being* can be anyone, anything, any time.

What do we do with all that space? What do we do with our computer screens? We put a screensaver on them: a sunset or a picture of our friends, or children. We usually choose something that has to do with us. If we're given a picture frame, we don't usually put in a picture of someone or something that means nothing to us. We might leave it blank, but if we don't, what goes in comes from us.

*****

Can a Nazi tell the truth? I stumbled across this question in the course of my studies.

The first time I read Martin Heidegger's seminal work *Sein und Zeit* (Being and Time) it was, in many ways, an enlightening experience. My God! His concepts of how humans are in the world, how they are connected to each other, the hidden potential for Being that is in all of us – it sounded so much like what I'd been trying to grasp and say for so long. I devoured his writings. His thoughts helped me clarify and develop my own. His ideas were so big: Being-in-the-world; Being-with; What-we-can-be. To use his own terminology, his words allowed a lot of light to come in. Light that illuminated the space between the words. The bigger the words, the more abstract – and the more space: *Can-be* leaves a lot of room for interpretation, while *You are* or *They are* narrows it down considerably.

And because I saw this connection between what Heidegger said and what I was thinking-and-feeling, I felt I understood him. Or, to be more precise, I felt he understood me. We all know that feeling: when someone has said things we would like to have said. The recognition: Yes, that's it. I quoted Heidegger in my publications and to my students to clarify what I wanted to say.

When it happens, this flash of re-cognition, you can't make it go away. It's happened, and it's there. You can't un-recognise things.

After a while, I didn't just read Heidegger, I read about him. And learned he had been a member of the National Socialist Party. That he admired Hitler. That he never apologised for or went back on his support for the objectives of National Socialism. Etc. Etc.

What does one do? Does the fact that Heidegger embraced National Socialist ideals until the end of his life invalidate anything that he said in his philosophical writings? All of it? Should I just ignore this hardly insignificant fact of his life? Carry on regardless and act (and think) as if it were irrelevant?

I can't do it. Yes, there were perhaps mitigating circumstances. None of us can know whether Heidegger accepted an influential post at Freiburg University to advance National Socialist thinking, or to combat it. We cannot know whether he really turned his back on his teacher, Edmund

Variations: No. 4

Husserl (who was Jewish and banned from the university), or whether he tried to help him. None of us can know what constraints, restraints, wishes or fears make a person act the way they do, especially in times of crisis.

But, the fact remains that, until his death in 1976, Heidegger had ample opportunity to distance himself from National Socialist ideology, and he never did.

Another stone to kick. I can't pretend it's not there. When this stone hit me, I was stunned. What did it mean? What could I do? Would I have to un-think Heidegger? How?

Well, you can't un-think things. You can't pretend you don't know them. But you can re-think them, re-order the facts in the light of new evidence. What did it mean for Heidegger's concept of Truth, that he subscribed to Nazi ideology? I had taken his view of Truth as the entirety of Being to embrace humanity. To allow for the unfolding of the potential inherent in all of us. Was I wrong? I don't know. What I do know, is that this aspect of Heidegger that I hadn't seen before – his membership of the Nazi Party – shed a new light on him and on the meaning of what he says. The spaces between his words are now overshadowed with foreboding. And I don't want to take the risk of partaking in it.

We can close our eyes to the light that illuminates space. Not seeing is one thing. Looking away is another. It requires an act of will.

I cannot un-think how Heidegger's words have influenced my own. They're there, in me. But I do not know what he meant, how he filled his space. I only know how I did. His life story suggests that my interpretation of the space he created with his words was wrong.

This is what Heidegger himself said:

...philosophy must [not] put forward correct and valid propositions, but [...] seeks beings in their unhiddenness as beings.

This is what genuine positive freedom offers; it is not only freedom *from* but freedom *for*.

...the essence of freedom is [...] the *illuminating* view: to allow [...] a light to come on and to bind oneself to this.

What this means is not a matter for further *talking*, but rather for *doing*. It should be said, however, that even to make a beginning with philosophy one must rid oneself of the illusion that man could pose let alone solve a problem, *without* some standpoint. The desire to philosophize from the standpoint of standpointlessness [...] is either childish [...] or disingenuous. [...] No freedom from any standpoint (something fantastic) but the right choice of standpoint, the courage to a standpoint, the setting in action of a standpoint and the holding out within it, is the task; ... .

Heidegger's action during and after the war makes it clear which standpoint he held out in. His standpoint as he lived it does not stand up to the rigours of his philosophy.

'What is spoken is never, and in no language, what is said.' The words that Heidegger spoke – or wrote – seem at odds with what he said, or meant. He writes 'Truth happens', and draws our attention to Pascal's distinction between the logic of the heart '... as ... against the logic of calculating reason'. On the same page he tells us that 'The widest orbit

Variations: No. 4

of being becomes present in the heart's inner space'. Is this space reserved only for the chosen few? Who chooses?

Can you believe in a National Socialist world order and still love humanity? The two patterns of order seem incompatible to me. I cannot yet see how they fit together. Heidegger's silence on his National Socialist leanings is not empty. It is not nothing.

*****

Picture courtesy of Birtukaine, Ethiopia, and *Light for the World*

What do you see in the picture? A house, a flower, a cat, a sun, another house. Children don't usually draw space – they draw objects that just float in the picture. This means that the objects are not connected to each other: They are just there. There is no visible relation between them. Each object is just shown as itself.

One way of representing space in painting is the use of light. Objects appear nearer or farther away according to the light they are painted in, more distant objects receding into greyness, for example. Light and colour as an expression of space are at the same time an expression of unity. They relate objects to each other.

Space is the medium which holds everything together. Light and space are shown by means of colour and objects and, at the same time, are the elements which lend colours and objects a particular feel or expression. As with sound in music, it is the space in-between which creates order, that tells us what we see, hear or feel.

That's why *Thank you* can mean *I'm in love*.

In Elizabeth Gaskell's novel, *North* and *South*, the manufacturer John Thornton harbours a secret passion for the heroine, Margaret Hale. After she moves away from the town where he lives, he misses her sorely, but cannot talk to anyone of what he is going through. One of his workers, Nicholas Higgins, asks him in conversation whether he's heard from Miss Hale at all. Upon which Thornton replies that Yes, he has had some business dealings with her. She's well... He then utters the words: *Thank you, Higgins*. Just a couple of words of common politeness.

It's funny, isn't it, how two little words can tell the story of your heart?

Variations: No. 4

If Thornton were indifferent to Margaret, he would not have thanked Higgins for inquiring after her welfare. We only say *Thank you* if the person whose health is being asked after means something to us. This automatic response in Thornton prompts Higgins to tell him more about what he knows of Margaret's personal life, and brings about a turning-point in their love story. Thornton himself remains unaware of what he has said with the words he has spoken.

What the film business calls the *backstory* always comes through. And a good screenplay will always let the actors do just what Elizabeth Gaskell let John Thornton do: make their emotional life-story shine through the words, without spelling it out. Because this is how we all 'act'.

As E.M. Forster put it: Emotion is not the theme, it is the central glow. We may not go around telling all and sundry the story of our lives, but, like John Thornton's, it slips out all the same. We all have a backstory, and it's there for all to see.

It wasn't John Thornton's words that told Higgins of his feelings for Margaret. It was the space around them. It was what he did not say, that was brought out into the open by what he did say. And, yes, the space was also filled by Higgins' knowledge, or hunch, that there might be something between Thornton and Margaret. He brought his own story into the space, filled it with his view, his own order of things too.

Just like light in painting, it is the space created by words that relates them to us and makes meaning. Words show us that the space is there. They shape it, hint at what might be in it, at where we could look and what we could feel. Words allow room for what we cannot, or do not want to say, to nevertheless be told.

> We cannot grasp things, or say things, quite as easily as we are led to believe. Most things cannot be put into words; They happen in a space which no word has ever entered...
>
> Rainer Maria Rilke, *Letter to Franz Xaver Kappus*
> 17th February 1903

Words, like painting and music, are not about *things*. They are about us, our lives, our backstory. What we mean, what we feel, is always the central theme. Our so-called inner life, the one we actually live and feel and experience, is what comes through. We can, after all, only 'express', 'put out' there, what is inside us. If we don't express what is inside us, we cannot put anything into our words or into the space between them. They remain hollow, and the space is empty. They cannot relate to anything, not even themselves, except on a very superficial level. What we say cannot ring true. Because it is divorced from our lived and emotional truth. All that anyone can understand is then merely the surface form. They cannot relate to what we're saying, because there is no where that they can bring themselves in and be with us.

The words we use are like the artist's 'subject matter' – they are simply the medium by which we reveal an inner meaning. And, like the artist or the musician, our inner meaning is how we experience life. Our words express the inexpressible. They carry our silence.

Variations: No. 5

Do you remember the first time you fell and cut your knee? You cried, somebody picked you up, said *There, there* and kissed it better. Perhaps they dabbed at the wound and put a plaster on it. What made you feel better? The plaster, or the kiss?

If you hadn't fallen over, you'd have probably continued to skip along and your parents would have watched affectionately from afar. It's the cut that made them rush up and take you in their arms. Your knee still hurt, but you got a hug in return.

We're all systems of flesh and blood. When we cut our knee, it bleeds. Our body sends out blood to wash out the wound. It knows what to do to get things back in order: A film forms over the gap, the skin starts to grow together and the tissue underneath it begins to heal. All these are automatic processes in a healthy body. Every time a disturbance occurs in the delicate balance of chemical, neurological and other processes that keep our body functioning, it knows how to get it back onto an even keel. Sometimes this happens very quickly, sometimes it takes a bit longer. Everything that happens in our bodies is finely tuned to restore order and harmony whenever anything is out of sync.

The whole system is maintained in functioning order by producing the appropriate reactions to disorder. It is the continuous re-adjustment to change and the disruption of harmony that keeps the whole thing going. If the system can't do that, it falls into dis-order, it becomes dis-eased. People have known this for a long time.

Variations: No. 5

The second century healer and philosopher, Galen of Pergamon, physician to the emperor Marcus Aurelius, defined disbalance or pain as the separation of that which naturally belongs together, in equilibrium: He called it *solutio continuitatis*, or the *dissolution of unity*. When the elements of our body are in disharmony, we feel dis-ease. But for Galen, as for Aristotle before him, the body was intricately woven to the soul. Indeed, it was the soul that was the driving force, that animated the body and made it alive.

Disease is not only a thing of the body, because the body is not only flesh and blood. If the body can be in disorder, so too can the soul. When we are torn asunder from what is part of us, it hurts: We are *home-sick, love-sick, sick at heart*. Balance, harmony, bringing back together restores our well-being.

Modern science brings evidence with more modern theories. We now *know* that, in many ways, Galen was right. The *psyche* – the soul – does affect the *soma* – the body. Emotional pain is processed in the same way as physical pain. If we don't feel that we belong, our physical health suffers. If we don't have anybody to kiss us better, it hurts more.

This isn't just because we're all incurable softies. We really were made that way. We know that the ability to feel with another person is part of our biological make-up. Modern science can tell us, can provide evidence that communion, sharing the reality of our lives with other people, isn't just romantic poetic stuff. It is real – and *really* necessary. Science can explain why, in the words of W. H. Auden, *we must love one another, or die*.

What science cannot do, is tell us that this is so. We know it if we live it, if we feel it. Science can explain, can tell us why. But it is art that re-awakens this knowing in us. It stirs what we know in our bones, the soul knowledge, that is stored in our bodies.

Science can exhibit pieces of evidence. To put them together, to see the connections, we need imagination, inspiration, passion. New discoveries, new insights, are the result of re-ordering and re-viewing the evidence. We see new things when we place them in a different relation to each other, when the light falls differently and the space between them is given new shape. Passion ignites the flash of recognition that made Archimedes shout *Eureka*! Science without the spark of passion is like collecting stones higgledy-piggledy and staring at them in confusion.

Science gives us a rational analysis. Infuse it with passion, and it is on the brink of art. The two are not worlds apart; they inhabit the same reality. They are manifestations of the emotional imperative to understand. They just create a different order, and trace different patterns. Science tells us what we can know. Art reminds us that we do know.

*****

Passion. A word we all know the meaning of – or do we? We don't often think of a patient in a hospital bed as being passionate. That's because we blot out one half of the meaning. *Patient* and *passionate* mean the same thing: suffering. The Passion of Christ is His suffering on the cross. Passion is pain. It becomes joyous when it moves us to find a release from the pain. The need to escape pain, whether of the soul or the body, is the force that propels what is inside us out into the open.

Variations: No. 5

> What is it that urges me
> To spill out my heart?
> I do not want your pity
> Nor your help
> Nor to confess what I have done.
> And yet I still disclose
> All my passions and my fears
>
> After Louis Aragon, *Les Poètes*

A cry in pain is a cry in pain. We don't stop to ask if it comes from a broken knee or a broken heart. At least, I hope not.

The Tower of Babel is an emotional truth. We are scattered, and we are confused. Our unity is dissolved, and we seek to restore it.

Wassily Kandinsky explained that the artist's creative impulse must be obedient to his own need:

> The artist... must watch only the trend of the inner need, and hearken to its words alone. ... The voice of the soul will in some degree at least make itself heard.

The voice of the soul always makes itself felt. We all see the world differently and give expression to our inner need. It's just that some people do it with more intent of purpose than others. We are all artists: Each of us sees the world differently. We all create our own reality and show it to others. We hearken to its words. The inner need urges us all to express ourselves.

The reality we express is the world that we know. We can only know the world through what is familiar to us. It is only through our particular, individual world that we can connect with the world of others, with what is universal. Not the other way round. We have our own child, and learn what it is to love children. We find affinity with all parents. We know what it means to be a mother, a father, one of a kind.

Vera Brittain, in her memoirs of the First World War, wrote how she was able to tend to wounded German soldiers. She stopped seeing them as the Enemy. Her own brother, her fiancé and her friends were also at the front, suffering, perhaps dying. Her love for them made her see the Germans as young men away from home who needed her affection and her care. She learned to see what else they could be, and what they were. She made the connection between the young Germans and the young men that she herself loved.

*****

> She and Mr. van der Luyden were so exactly alike that Archer wondered how, after forty years of the closest conjugality, two such merged identities ever separated enough for anything as controversial as a talking over.
>
> Edith Wharton, *The Age of Innocence*

When we understand each other as much as Luisa and Henry van der Luyden, we come to a standstill. Nothing happens between us, because there is no in-between. If we become one with another person, we can no longer come together.

Can we understand too much?
My wife doesn't understand me...
Maybe the best answer to that old line is: *Lucky you...*

Variations: No. 5

Humberto Maturana has described how we all, as living systems, need to meet to be reminded again and again of who we are – and who we are not. No system functions in a vacuum; it needs others to define its own borders. We systems of flesh and blood need to come together so that each of us can remain separate. So that we know who we are. We need to come together *because* we are separate. So that we can be seen for what we are. Maturana – biologist, systems theorist and humanist – sums up the pain, the complexity and the excitement that this causes in one word: Love.

*****

Words always single out specific things and specific characteristics of things. A *blue sky*. But where does the sky stop and the sea start? And the sky is not only blue, it is white, and yellow, and red... As with Manet's *Asparagus*, we can't see it all. And like Chopin's Prelude, we can't name it all. But it is there. Words light up the space that they are in. They show us there is more – if we care to look.

Mary could be – and is – also Isolde; a soldier is also a son; bath-night could be any night of the week. Mum could also be Audrey Hepburn. *Auf Wiedersehen* is also *Be seein' ya*, is *Au revoir*, is *Hope we'll meet again*, is *Enchanté*, is *Delighted to meet you...*

*****

Words, in any language, etch out patterns in the reality we live in. There is only one. And that is why we can each have our own way of living it, looking at it, and naming it. Whether English, Urdu or Irish, all words in all languages help us see parts of the same reality. They are all part of the same space. And each one is related to the other by virtue of this space. It is the unifying element.

A word, like a blue butterfly, can show us what has always been there, but we've never seen. It can fly away, fade into space. But we know it's there. The space isn't empty; it's full of butterflies waiting to be seen.

Variations: No. 6

Stoned, Jakob Ritt

Why is a feeling like a stone?

Because it can hit you.

Because it has the force of nature behind it.

Because, even if it's very tiny, you always know it's there.

Because it can collide with other ones.

Because once it hits you, it leaves a mark.

If you pretend it's not there, you'll stumble over it.

Other people can see and hear and touch it, too.

Because it's a hard fact.

Because it obeys the laws of nature.

And we all know there are lots of them around.

Variations: No. 6

The difference is: You can kick a stone.
                    You can't kick a feeling.

*****

How true is all this? What proof do we have? Can we say *You know what I mean* with the same certainty as E=mc² ?

We know that the need to communicate is an innate human urge.

We know that communication means sharing how we experience the world; sharing our reality, our take on things.

This sharing, this communion, can take many forms: painting, music, a touch, a look, art, science – and language.

Language, using words, is one way of sharing what we live through with others.

We know that sometimes we know what people are getting at.

And sometimes we don't. Whether it's art, music, poetry – or just plain everyday talking.

We know it's not what you say, it's how you say it.

And: What you don't say.

We know when people mean what they say. Or if they're just mouthing the words.

We know it's easier to understand if we've 'been there' too.

And we know when we've been understood, when someone else has seen us.

It's not about the words.

We all know that.

If it were about the words, we'd all know what we meant.

If it were just about the words, we'd never give ourselves away – we'd always know what we were saying.

If words were all-important, there would be nothing between the lines.

Or behind the words.

We would only be *saying* things and could not *mean* them.

If it were just about the words, we'd never be able to put things into our own words.

We have no proof. Except our experience. We know that these things happen, are true, because we have lived them.

All the scientific evidence is a back-up.

It tells us: Yes, this is plausible. It makes logical sense. Which helps. It helps for the very reason communication takes place: It re-affirms what we know because other people see it that way too.

Variations: No. 6

The need for communication is a fact of life.

The need to understand is a fact of life.

Not-understanding is a fact of life.

Revealing our inner life, our emotional truth, through what we say, is inevitable.

It is inevitable, because that's what language is there for. Communication is an emotional imperative.

Whether in art, or science, or language – the backstory is always the reason why we understand. It determines where we stand, where we look, what we see.

The facts of our lives are the things that we put into words. And into the silence in-between.

No, we cannot say *You know what I mean*, or *I know what you mean* with the same certainty as $E=mc^2$. There are no logical equations to show that *this* means *that*. There can never be equations of meaning, because no two people can ever mean the same thing. Not even if they use the same words.

We don't have the same certainty. We have more uncertainty. More space for interpretation, and thus also for error.

Uncertainty gives us the space to not-understand so that we can learn to understand each other. It gives us space for imagination, for us to let other people in, and for them to bring themselves in. Certainty? No. Precision? No. Exactitude is not the same as truth.

We can never be certain that we understand someone else. But we can be sure enough to give it a try. And the trying, the getting to grips with what somebody else could mean, is the purpose of the exercise. The uncertainty is what keeps the whole thing going. Of that we can be certain.

The other certainty, is, of course, the things that we know because they cannot be told.

Variations: No. 7

To promote understanding between people, cultures and nations. I wish I could say that's why I became a translator. But, no. I became a translator because I needed a job. And because I needed to figure out what made people not understand me – even when I used the right words. I needed to learn how to translate myself.

So, was it all worth it? Have I answered any of my questions? Why don't we understand each other? Why does not-understanding hurt? What does *understand* mean?

I've learnt that feelings are facts. We know what we know. Descartes was not necessarily wrong: *I think, therefore I am.* But that is only part of the picture. The other part is feeling what we are, and feeling what we know. Emotionality and rationality are not mutually exclusive, but complementary. The heart has its reasons, which reason has no access to. As Pascal reminds us: It is not rationality that binds us to others; the very idea is absurd. It is not merely a philosophical argument that reason and 'the heart' belong together. The two are biologically inseparable. They are so for the very pragmatic reason that we need them both to survive. You can't have one without the other because neither would make evolutionary sense without the other. Again, Pascal sums it up for us: There are two extremes: excluding reason, and admitting only reason. We all know that.

Scientists know that too. If you have a hunch and the facts don't fit, well, then the facts are wrong. You keep on looking. Of course, it's not the

Variations: No. 7

facts that are wrong, its the way you've been looking at them, the order you placed them in. Or maybe you've been looking for the wrong facts. Change the pattern, and they might fit better. If we left our feelings out of the picture, we'd just give up.

The story of the Tower of Babel tells an emotional truth: We do not understand each other. We are scattered on the face of the earth, and we are confounded. Science can corroborate the truth.

Was it worth it? Have I learned anything new? Maybe not. But I've learned to look at things newly. And to feel them newly. We don't say what we mean. And we don't mean what we say. It's not the words that matter.

We will never understand each other. Not-understanding has to hurt, because otherwise we wouldn't try to put a stop to it. We put our words out there. *Our* words – not somebody else's. We want people to know what our words mean, because we want them to see who we are. I knew all that when I was five. And so did you.

So where does that get me?

Now I know what I know. And I haven't just got back-up. I've got lots of different angles on what I know. That helped me know it better, to know more. 'My thing' is a real Thing; other people see it too. They just call it different names.

Worth it? If you think what you feel, and feel what you think, it brings you full circle: You can only recognise what you already know.

Variations: No. 7

Fifty years of wondering why, to come up with this: We need to be in touch with each other. Words create the space between us, that keeps us apart and keeps us connected.

Fifty years to get back to where I started from: *People don't understand each other. But sometimes we do.*

Worth it? Yep. Because now I know why. Language arises out of our inexpressible, individual, universal longing. It sometimes goes wrong. It has to, so that it can get better again. It has to tear us apart, so that we can come closer. It must remind us that we are alone, so that we remember we are not alone. We have the gift of speech so that we can say the things that there are no words for. I have, for the moment, escaped the pain of not understanding.

Knowing why, understanding, means I can stop getting angry, or hurt, when people don't understand. I can make sense of it. Dis-order stops being dis-ease. Understanding means fitting it into my scheme of things, really taking it in. What we understand becomes part of us.

Of course, the circle is never complete, never quite exact. Whether in painting, art, science, language, music, or any other form of human communication, harmony will always be a fragile, temporary, tenuous affair. Perfect order is not a feature of life. It is the beginning of the end. The more we understand, the more gaps we see in the picture. And the disorder starts again. Things move. Life lives.

Variations: No. 7

We are always walking the tightrope between understanding and not-understanding. Between harmony and confusion. We could fall off the tightrope any minute. And we do. The Tower of Babel happened. We all lost our innocence. But we can all get it back – at least for a moment. We can always get back on the high-wire – or, at least, we can try. The excitement lies in the uncertainty.

We are all translators. Some more, some less. Some of us do it for a living. We all do it, because we live.

Circle, Michèle Cooke, 2011

As you can see, my circle is far from perfect.

Some bits are more definite than others – and some decidedly sketchy. Well, I never did claim to be Giotto. But the circle is round, more or less. Exactitude is not the same thing as truth. This is the circle I've come up with for now. Can't wait to see how the next one turns out.

Variations: No. 8

Here are some words that Rainer Maria Rilke, a struggling poet, wrote to a younger struggling poet:

> I ask you, dear friend, to have patience with all that is unresolved in your heart. I ask you to try to love the unanswered questions, the way we love what is behind doors we have not yet opened, and as we love books written in a language we cannot yet understand. Do not go looking for the answers; they cannot be given to you, for you cannot yet live them. And we must learn to live everything, to live all that we have been given. So let yourself live the questions. And perhaps one day you will start to live the answers. Perhaps even now you have within you what you need to shape and build; [...]
> Learn how to live this life; try to live it. And accept what comes in complete trust...
>
> Rainer Maria Rilke, Letter to Franz Xaver Kappus
16 July, 1903

Poet, artist, Chopin, Mary ... same difference.

Variations: No. 9

How far is it to Heaven? Every time Eddie the maintenance man looked at his life through someone else's eyes, he had to refocus his own picture, re-scramble the pieces of the puzzle, and put them in a different order. Every time he understood someone else's life, he learned to accept more of his own. He saw again what he already knew, but in a different light, and with a different knowledge. He lived his life again and again, each time in a new flash of recognition. And seeing the lives of those he loved through their eyes, he learned that their truth was part of his.

There was never only one picture that held the whole truth. As Eddie learned to understand his violent, unpredictable father, he lost his fear of him and learned to love him. As he understood his wife's fears and insecurities, he stopped feeling guilty and could love her more freely.

The people in Eddie's heaven were all, in some way, part of his backstory. One of them went back to many years before he was born. How far does our backstory go? At what point can we *say I've understood enough*? For Eddie, it was five people. But then, he was in heaven. Here on earth, we say it again and again because, for better and worse it's never enough for long. There's no happy ending. Or lots of them. Depends on how you look at it.

Whichever way: The story goes on and on.

Finale

Monsieur Bouvard and Monsieur Pécuchet were two middle-aged men who lived in Paris, and who fell in love. Gustave Flaubert told their story in his last, unfinished novel. Bouvard – big, bold and florid – and timid little Pécuchet happen to sit down at the same time on the same bench one hot summer afternoon. They both take off their hats at the same time and place them top-down on the seat beside them. They get into conversation, and spend the evening together. They go for a meal, and meet again the very next day.

> It was clear that something momentous had happened.
> From the very beginning, they were knit together by threads no eye can see. For, after all, who can say what draws us to one another? Why do quirks and foibles, in one man, incite indignation, or mere indifference and yet, in another, enrapture and enchant us? What is called the lightning flash kindles all the human passions.

Love at first sight? Pécuchet sees in Bouvard's upturned hat that he, too, has written his name inside. In that one moment, the two men recognised each other, saw in the other something of himself. Very brief. Very humdrum: a name-band in a hat. But enough for their worlds to touch. And this fleeting touch forges between them a deep and lasting bond which years of hardship, failure and disappointment fail to destroy. In habit, appearance, character and taste, Bouvard and Pécuchet are as different as two people can be. They laugh with each other, tease each other and, as the years go by, hurt and annoy each other. But the bond remains unbroken. All it took was a lightning flash, a *coup de foudre*.

Finale

No, it's not a love-story in the conventional sense. Not romantic love. But it is love.

The lightning flash that gives us a glimpse into another's world shows that it is also ours. It might reveal only a slim, slender cusp, or light up infinite vistas of mutual recognition. It could last for ever, or be gone in an instant. Whenever realities meet, they touch. The lightning flash kindles all the human passions.

Flaubert often spent weeks in search of just the right word, *le mot juste*, which would say it all. None of us will ever get it just right. The words we use can only ever be right for us. But if they resonate with our own truth, they are likely to touch on that of others. And yet, we will never see just what another person means, because, whenever we understand, we also have to not-understand. That is, of course, unless we get to Eddie's heaven. Which is a great place to be – when you're dead. Until then, we need the lightning flash. It tears us apart, and brings us together.

Not even Flaubert could say it all. There is no perfect word. Who needs perfect?

Lightning strikes again and again. In many different ways, and for many different reasons. It kindles all the human passions.

> *Le coup de foudre est vrai pour toutes les passions.*

Flaubert's words sound the depths of what each of us knows. As near perfect as you can get.

Encore I: Caprice

I'm very glad I didn't get to heaven when I was five. But you probably got that already.

Encore II: Caprice

It turns out, I wasn't really French. By the time I got to nineteen I knew I had to give up on the long legs. And adding the chic little *accent* to my name, Michèle, didn't help much.

But I did live in Paris for a while.
And I'm still working on the pearls and the Balmain...

Thank you

I must first thank my publishers, Peter Lang, for their patience in allowing this book to grow past several optimistic deadlines.

Sincere thanks to Georges Moustaki and Polydor Records for kind permission to use the lyrics from *Ma Solitude*.

I am grateful to Rupert Roniger and Gabriel Müller of Light for the World, Austria, for kindly allowing me to use the painting for January in their Children's Calendar 2011 and to Birtukaine for her generous contribution.

Danke, to my students, for keeping me on my toes.

Many people have, in their own different way, shared the process of writing this book with me:

My son, Daniel

Eileen Benson	Herbert Kaiser
Grainne Carty	André Lequet
Philip Casey	Doireann McHugh
Elaine Clear	Vera Novotny
Gail Cooke	Georg Raslagg
Karen Fletcher	Anna Reiner
Halina Froudist	Renate Resch
Angelika Hirsch	Ursula Russell
Michael Huter	Aurelia Windhager
Dan Hogan	

Thank you, every one of you.

And Rowland, for all the things I can't put into words...

To the best of the author's knowledge, all quotations included here fall under the fair use or public domain guidelines of copyright law in the European Union.

All quotations remain the intellectual property of their respective originators. The author does not assert any claim of copyright for individual quotations. All quotations have been fully cited and attributed to their original author.

In quoting others the author does not in any way mean to imply the endorsement or approval of said originators in relation to the book or its contents.

Where possible, full permission has been obtained from the appropriate copyright holder.

Back-up notes

Foreword, pages 9-10

Erwin Schrödinger has this to say about the way science presents how the world is:

The scientific world-picture vouchsafes a very complete understanding of all that happens – it makes it just a little too understandable [...] the scientific world-view contains of itself no ethical values, no aesthetical values, not a word about our own ultimate scope or destination, ...

Schrödinger 1954 (1996), p.96-97

... a moderately satisfying picture of the world has only been reached at the high price of taking ourselves out of the picture, stepping into the role of a non-concerned observer.

Schrödinger 1958 (2008), p.119

A strange reality! Something seems to be missing in it.

Schrödinger 1958 (2008), p.58

See also Marilynne Robinson (2010) on why we need to remember the inner self and Martha Nussbaum (2010) on how we need the humanities to put ourselves back in the picture.

*****

Prelude, page 14

Mitch Albom, *the five people you meet in Heaven.*

*****

Impromptus: No. 4, pages 29-30

Why do we listen to sad music? Is it because it makes us feel sad, or because it speaks to us of a shared experience? (See Stephen Davies' discussion of the subject, 1997.) If it is a purging of emotion – catharsis – we must ask ourselves why and how. Catharsis gives us relief in the broadest sense of the word: *The removal, or partial removal of any evil, or of anything oppressive or burdensome, by which some ease is obtained; succor; alleviation; comfort; ease* (Webster's New International

Back-up notes

Dictionary, 2nd edition, 1957). Knowing that others have partaken of a common experience makes it lighter for us. See also Aristotle's *Poetics* on the universality of emotion (5.5, p.16) and Malcolm Heath on catharsis in Aristotle's *Politics* (1996, p.xxvii).

Impromptus: No. 4, pages 30-31
For a discussion of the relation between music and emotion see, for example, Karl/Robinson 1997; Levinson 1997; Meyer 1956; Thomspon 2009, especially chapter 6.

For a discussion of translating opera texts and how words need to blend in with the music, see, for example, Kaindl 1995.

*****

Impromptus: No. 6, page 37
L'enfer, c'est les autres. Jean-Paul Sartre, in *Huis clos.*

*****

Impromptus: No. 7, pages 39-40
George Sand, who was Chopin's lover for nine years or so, wrote in her autobiography her version of how Chopin came to compose the 'Raindrop' Prelude, and how incensed he was that anyone should presume to regard his music as mere imitation of other circumstances and thus fail to appreciate the subtlety of his expression. (*Histoire de ma vie*, vol. XIII, Paris 1855. Quoted in Reich 1959, p.179f)

Franz Liszt thought the Raindrop name referred to Prelude No.8 F minor, but expert opinion has now fixed on No.15, D flat major. Other preludes were also variously named, according to interpretation, for example Prelude No.1 C major was named *Réunion* or *Attente fiévreuse de l'aimée*. (Translated as *Reunion* or *Waiting feverishly for the beloved.* See Reich 1959, p.180f.) Again, the names do not come from Chopin himself.

Chopin believed in appealing directly to the listeners' sensation and 'suspending for a while the stimulation of [...] intellect. Almost alone among the Romantics of his generation, Chopin showed little interest in linking his music to pictorial, literary or autobiographical subjects...' (Stanley Sadie 1980, p.306).

Back-up notes

See Pitrou 1950, p.91f and Kallberg 1996, p.135f on the composition of the Preludes and p.161f on Chopin's image in the music market.

Impromptus: No. 8, pages 43-44

Van Gogh painted eight pairs of shoes. According to Martin Heidegger who, it is thought, discussed the shoes painted in 1886 (see Schapiro 1998), the work describes the equipmental nature of the shoes and what this equipment is in truth. As Schapiro points out, Heidegger overlooks the 'personal and physiognomic' nature of the shoes and what it is in them that touched the artist (p.430). The shoes are not just an instrument of use but a part of the artist's self. This was corroborated by Gauguin, who shared van Gogh's quarters in Arles (p.431). '...for van Gogh, the shoes [...] were a piece of his own life.' (p.431). However, Jacques Derrida, in the same volume, takes issue with Schapiro's critique of Heidegger's discussion of van Gogh's shoes and quotes Cézanne's dictum: 'I owe you the truth in painting' (p.432). The question is: Which truth? And whose truth? I suggest, with Schapiro, that it is the artist's emotional truth, which he puts out for others to see and to share.

See also Mark Rothko's discussion of truth and emotion (2004, p.14f, 34f, 76f).

Art need be neither mimesis, nor catharsis. It is enough for it to 'produce excitement in co-existence' (William Wordsworth, quoted in Berlyne 1971, before preface, no page number) and to serve the communicative function of sharing values. This meets the emotional and somatic requirement of providing information beyond that required for mere physical nourishment, but that nevertheless reinforces individual as well as collective identity and social cohesion. (See Berlyne 1971, p.59f) 'Some kind of aesthetic activity is [...] a feature of all the 3000 or so cultures that are to be found on the earth's surface. This suggests strongly that art grows out of some fundamental characteristics of the human nervous system.' (Berlyne 1971, p.27)

Henri Matisse: *L'exactitude n'est pas la vérité*. Quoted in Herbert Read 1959, p.44 and Alfred Barr 1951, p.128, 253, 561.

*****

Back-up notes

Variations: No. 1, page 53
Giorgio Vasari, *Lives of the Artists*, written 1550-1568, quoted from the 1965 translation, 1987 edition, p.64.

Variations: No. 1, page 54
See Ames-Lewis 2000, p.10-11 on the inaccuracy of much of Vasari's testimony.

Variations: No. 1, page 55
Le Petit Prince (The Little Prince) by Antoine de Saint-Exupéry.

Variations: No. 1, page 56
Astonishingly, until quite recently, grandmothers were regarded as an evolutionary 'anomaly'. They shouldn't really be here, since they have no 'evolutionary' (i.e. reproductive) function. But scientists finally realised there must be a better explanation. And, of course, there is one: to help nurture the young and foster social bonding. See Kristen Hawkes 2003 and 2004; Elaine Morgan 1972; and Robin Dunbar 1996 on why nature gave us grandmothers.

Birds adapt the way they 'speak' to where they live. Even members of the same species don't all speak the same language. See, for example, Baker/Cunningham 1958; Kroodsma 2005 and Luther/Baptista 2010.

Hitler and grammar: We all know that language shapes the way we think, and whether we think in verbs, nouns or adjectives has an effect on how we perceive things. For a discussion of the connection between nominalisation and totalitarian ideology, see Variations No. 3 & 4 and the notes to pages 67-68.

In German, academics are called *Wissenschaftlerin*, if they are women, and *Wissenschaftler*, if they are men. *Wissen* is one of the German words for *knowing*. A *Wissenschaftlerin* is a person who wants to know.

The English word *science* also means *to know*, or *distinguish from* (Latin: *sciens*, present participle of *scire*, Websters Third New International Dictionary.)

Variations: No. 1, pages 56-57
Scientific objectivity is in fact inter-subjective consensus. The more one's peers agree with one's findings, the more it is accepted as truth.

Scientific knowledge is a process of communication and social construction. See, for example Jerome Bruner, *Acts of meaning,* 1990. Science is an act of meaning and as such is not simply information. 'Information is indifferent with respect to meaning.' (p.4) There is not '...only one way of constructing meaning, or one right way.' (p.30) See also Paul Feyerabend, on the authority of the sciences, 1978, p.102f; Karin Knorr-Cetina, on the fabrication of knowledge, 1984 and epistemic cultures, 1999 and Niklas Luhmann on science as a system of communication, 1990.

*****

Variations: No. 2, pages 60-61
This urge to establish connections between things is common to all forms of life. All living things have to make sense of the world they are living in to be able to orient themselves, to know what to expect, and to find their own place in the world. This can be instinctively and unconsciously, as when a frog knows that flies are likely to buzz by and that they have something to do with him and his tongue, or as a process of reflection, as when humans ponder the meaning of life. For a discussion of how animals make sense of the world by seeing what relates to them, see, for example, Uexküll/Kriszat 1970.

Seeing things in new connections, new patterns and thus new forms of order is inherently linked with surprise.

Metaphor makes new connections. In other words, it suggests that something is like something else, e.g. ruby red lips, the wild romantic sea, the bloom of youth. It is the juxtaposition of hitherto unconnected things. That is one of the reasons why Aristotle recommends metaphor as a valuable rhetorical tool; he speaks of its *'clarity, pleasantness* and *unfamiliarity'* (*Rhetoric,* Ch.3.2, p.219, original emphasis). Metaphor reveals hitherto unseen characteristics and causes recognition between related but not obvious things. (*Rhetoric,* Ch.3.10, p.235 and Ch.3.11, p.239). This sudden recognition of affinity (*Rhetoric,* Ch.3.2, p.220) and surprise engenders attention and interest. In the same way, simile produces 'swift understanding' and creates knowledge that is pleasant. (*Rhetoric,* Ch.3.10, p.235f; *Poetics,* Ch.9.4, p.37) Wit, metaphor and simile all promote understanding. See also Lawson Tancred's introduction to Aristotle's *Rhetoric,* p.40 and his discussion of the 'charm of unfamiliarity'.

Back-up notes

George Lakoff and Mark Johnson also pointed out the inherently metaphorical nature of language over thirty years ago. (Lakoff 1980 and 1986; Lakoff/Johnson 1980)

Variations: No. 2, page 62
See, for example, Dissanayake 2000; Fonagy 2001; Parker/Mitchell 1994; Stern 1985; Thompson 1990 on mother-infant interaction, imitation and the process of differentiation.

Even to say that we 'relate' to the world amounts to separating ourselves from it. We are not just 'part' of it, but of it. What I 'am' and what is 'outside' of me, 'surrounding' me, are continuous with each other: *res cogitans* and *res extensa* are made of the same stuff (Munz 1993, p.186; see also p.6f and Uexküll/Kriszat 1970, p.107f).

Schrödinger on the unity of the perceiving subject and perceived object:

> It is the same elements that go to compose my mind and the world. This situation is the same for every mind and its world [...]. The world is given me only once, not one existing and one perceived. Subject and object are only one. The barrier between them cannot be said to have broken down [...], for this barrier does not exist.
>
> Schrödinger 1958 (2008), p.127

See also Rudolf Arnheim's *Entropy and Art* (1971, especially p.23f), for a discussion of the continuity of matter.

Variations: No. 2, page 63
'Order is a necessary condition for anything the human mind is to understand.' (Arnheim 1971, p.1)

'Order is a prerequisite for survival ... the social organisations of animals, the spatial formations of travelling birds or fishes, the webs of spiders and bee-hives... .' (Arnheim 1971, p.3)

See also Arnheim 1971, p.13 on how disorder is the coming together of independent forms of order 'locked in unreadable conflict'.

*****

Back-up notes

Variations: No. 3, page 65

'I want, then simply
to say the names of things.'
Rainer Maria Rilke, *Book of Hours*, I,60
(Translation by Anita Barrows and Joanna Macy)

As Barrows and Macy point out in their introduction to the *Book of Hours* (p.29), Rilke wrote of our capacity to see the '...reality of the world [and] to redeem it through that act of transforming attention, which is naming – or love.'

Variations: No. 3, page 66

'The importance of labels is that they make us see the things we label *as if the label had not intervened.*' (Munz 1993, p.56)

Variations: No. 3, pages 67-68

See Anna Wierzbicka's discussion of the effects of nominalisation and other word categories on how we perceive the world (1988). Also Lakoff 1982 (1987) on categorisation and perception.

Words and names can be reclaimed. In other words, they can be taken back and given a new meaning. When Jewish people start up a magazine called *The Jew*, it means something different, it refers to different things than the anti-Semitic literature does. When black youths call each other *nigger*, it means a different thing from when a white person throws this word at them.

We are all trying to make a case for our own take on reality by the words we use. That's why we misunderstand each other – our realities clash. They have to, so that they can meet. Communication between interacting systems requires 'anti-communication' (Maturana 1978, p.54). Communion, or 'structural coupling' in Maturana's terminology (p.54f), must be preceded by the struggle to attain it.

Some of us have more power to force our reality on to more people. The discourse of the powerful determines the reality in which most people have to live. See, for example, Fairclough 1989 on the relation between language and power.

*****

Back-up notes

Variations: No. 4, page 72
See Will Eisner 1985, p.39f on the use of space to tell a story.
I am grateful to Marina Bilobrk, Sandra Horn and Gladysmay Regalado for drawing my attention to the meaning and function of space in comics.

Variations: No. 4, page 73
See also William Forde Thompson on music and silence (2009, p.78f) and Kendall Walton on music, imagination, fictional worlds and space (1997).

Variations: No. 4, pages 74-78
Martin Heidegger *Sein und Zeit* (*Being and Time*, 1926).
Being-in-the-world: In-der-Welt-sein
Being-with: Mit-Sein
What-we-can-be: Sein-Können (usual translation: 'potential-for-being')

In his introduction to the German edition of Victor Farías' documentation of Heidegger's involvement with National Socialism, Jürgen Habermas discusses how Heidegger's use of abstract nouns leaves almost too much room to interpret his meaning and amounts to disclaiming personal responsibility:

> Mit Hilfe einer Operation, die man 'Abstraktion durch Verwesentlichung' nennen könnte, gelingt so die Entkoppelung der Seinsgeschichte vom politisch-historischen Geschehen. [...] Heidegger hält sich wie stets im Allgemeinen auf. (1989, p.30)

However, while in no way condoning Heidegger's politics, Habermas is at pains to show that his philosophy can be appreciated in isolation from his political convictions. 'Zwischen Werk und Person darf kein kurzschlüssiger Zusammenhang hergestellt werden. Heideggers philosophisches Werk [...] verdankt seine Autonomie der Kraft seiner Argumente.' (p.34) He argues that it may be possible to read Heidegger's writing independently of its ideological context: 'Dann kann [...] ein produktiver Anschluss auch nur gelingen, wenn man sich auf die *Argumente* einlässt – und diese aus ihrem weltanschaulichen Kontext *heraushebt*.' (p.34, original emphasis)

Whether it is indeed possible to divorce what a person says from who he is without oneself veering, however inadvertently, towards an acceptance of his beliefs, is a crucial question. As will be clear from what I have written, I do not subscribe to this view.

Back-up notes

Heidegger's statements on philosophy are taken from his *Essence of Truth*: p.9; p.43, original emphasis; p.44, original emphasis; p.57, original emphasis.

'What is spoken is never, and in no language, what is said.' (Heidegger 1971, p.11)
'Truth happens' (Heidegger 1971, p.54)

Heidegger on Pascal's distinction between the logic of the heart '... as ... against the logic of calculating reason' (1971, p.125).

'The widest orbit of being becomes present in the heart's inner space.' (Heidegger 1971, p.125)

When we *know* something, it becomes literally incorporated, i.e. it becomes somatic knowledge. See, for example, Fichte (I 312-315, p.228-231) and Redding (1999, *passim*).

This is why we always bring our own knowledge into what other people say. What we understand is always as much a question of who we are as of who the other person is:

> The text, whether of prophet or poet, expands for what ever we can put into it...
> George Eliot, *Middlemarch*, Chapter 5

Variations: No. 4, pages 78-79
Space is filled, and space relates. See Mark Rothko (2004) on the use of space in painting, p.57, 31f and 56f on the use of light as a unifying medium, p.57f on how space is not empty and unites subjective sensation with objectivity.

Variations: No. 4, page 80
In his recommendations on how to write a good screenplay, Robert McKee (1998) advises that when '...we use a few selected details, the audience's imagination supplies the rest...' (p.188). Emotional authenticity is achieved by the well-known principle of 'show, don't tell' (p.334). Like Aristotle in his *Art of Rhetoric* (*passim*), McKee emphasises how honesty convinces us without, however, explicitly telling us what to think: '...never force words into a character's mouth to *tell* the audience about the world, [...] Rather, *show* us honest, natural scenes in which

human beings talk and behave in honest, natural ways [...] yet at the same time indirectly pass along the necessary facts.' (p.334, original emphasis). We all show, and don't tell.

E.M. Forster, 'Emotion is the central glow', from *The Prince's Tale and Other Uncollected Writings*, quoted in Ruth Padel 2007, p.xviii.

Variations: No. 4, page 81
To say that words are not about things sounds heretical. The denotative function of language is conventionally taken as a given: *Look out there's a sabre-tooth tiger on the horizon!*

However, if we look at the role of vocal and other forms of communication in other animals, especially primates, we see that language in the broadest sense has the primary function of alerting members of the same species to each other's emotional states. Letting others know that you are afraid, worried or happy is a survival advantage. It not only alerts them to danger, but also to your need for physical or emotional nurture.

Chimpanzees and other primates use grooming as a means of social bonding (see, for example, Geissmann 2000; Savage-Rambaugh 1988), and utter sounds to express closeness. See for example Robin Dunbar's discussion of how grooming and language have an evolutionary connection and serve to reinforce social cohesion, 1996 and Dunbar/Spoors 1995. Communication in the animal world does not only have a denotative function.

> Grooming [...] is the most common affirmative behaviour among primates [...] the primary function of grooming is to aid in establishing and maintaining close social bonds.
>
> Cheney/Seyforth 1990, p.36-37

Cheney and Seyforth also discuss how primates evaluate other individuals (p. 61), make friends (p.72), and relate to others by vocal and non-vocal communication (p.84, 88, 98f). Communication in primates clearly has to do with their emotional states:

> They [monkeys] behave as if predisposed to divide events in the world around them into broad categories that require a grunt, a scream, an alarm call, or no vocalization at all.
>
> Cheney/Seyforth 1990, p.138

There appears to be an evolutionary relation between human communication, human vocalization and the communication needs of other primates. (Cheney/Seyforth 1990, p.137) See also Richard Byrne's discussion of primates' having a theory of mind, being able to understand one another, and establishing social bonds, 1995, especially p.111f and 196f; Gomez 1994 and de Waal 2009, p.69f.

Moreover, from a systems theoretical perspective, denotation cannot be regarded as a primitive operation:

> Language must arise as a result of something else that does not require denotation for its establishment...
>
> Maturana 1978, p.50

Denotation must therefore be a by-product or side effect of something else: 'Denotation arises only [...] as an *a posteriori* commentary [...] about the consequences of operation of the interacting systems.' (Maturana 1978, p.50, emphasis added)

What then constitutes the survival advantage of human language? If language does not primarily provide information of the sabre-tooth tiger variety, it must give us some other, more important form of 'information'.

As Maturana points out: 'To understand the evolutionary origin of natural language requires the recognition of a basic biological process that could generate it.' (1978, p.53) Humans are biological beings. They interact with one another through their behaviour. Consequently, this behaviour must be fundamentally biological in nature.

Studies suggest that Broca's area, long thought to be dedicated exclusively to language use, is also the site of other tasks regarded as essential for social interaction. These include the work of mirror neurons which enable a 'neural map of an action [and] create a common link between the actor and the observer'. (Heiser et al 2003, p.1123) The imitation of motor tasks appears to be linked to language processing. This indicates

> ... an evolutionary continuity between action recognition, imitation and language, and shared neural mechanisms for all these forms of communication between individuals. These shared neural mechanisms [...] [create] a neural identity

between the sender and the receiver of communication that grounds understanding.

Heiser et al 2003, p.1128

Language processing has inherently to do with *relating to others like us*, sharing experience and knowing (or imagining) what the other person is going through.

The interaction of humans as biological systems is not simply the transmission of information for the purpose of instruction (Maturana 1978, p.54). Our interaction has to do with the state which each system is in (Maturana 1978, p.50). This state is an internal condition.

Watzlawick et al (1967) also pointed out the systemic character of human communication (*passim*), and the priority of the relationship level over 'content' (esp. p.23f, 51-54, 80-95, 129f, 214f). Although relationship is defined as a mathematical concept (p.22f), it is clear that what is at stake in human communication is the relationship between humans as interacting systems and the effects of this relating on their psychological (emotional) state.

'Information' about who and how we are is the point of the exercise. Everything that we live and feel is too deep for words. Meaning must be oblique, because there can be no single 'face value'. Words mean the lived and felt life that prompts them. When I say 'Hello ugly' to my son, he knows exactly what I mean because he has lived what I feel behind the words. Similarly, when John Keats writes

> The sedge has withered from the Lake
> And no birds sing
>
> *La belle dame sans merci*

in order to conjure up the utter bleakness of the landscape and the chill in the knight's soul, it does not matter that it is 'objectively' untrue that birds do not sing in the winter. What we call poetic license is the use of words to depict emotional truth. Literality is not the issue. And not just in poetry.

One reason why literal language is not understood is that it is seldom actually taken at 'face value'. What is spoken is not what is said. The illusion that it is words that carry meaning is subscribed to only when it is considered necessary or appropriate to mask the emotional truth behind them. It is only then that what is spoken is taken for what is said.

What is not spoken, the oblique meanings of what is uttered, rules and shapes much of our lives. Edith Wharton's *Age of Innocence* is all about the power of the unspoken to tell us what to think, to feel and to do. Newland Archer's separation from the woman he loves is effected through the silent conspiracy of his family to tell him what it knows:

> ...Archer felt like a prisoner in the centre of an armed camp. He looked about the table and guessed at the inexorableness of his captors [...] and a deathly sense of the superiority of implication and analogy over direct action, and of silence over rash words, closed in on him like the doors of the family vault.
>
> *Age of Innocence*, Chapter 32

Literal language also leaves little room for the imagination. Randy Olson, in his book *Don't be such a scientist*, advises us not to be 'so literal minded'. (2009, p.49f) The straightforward logic of science and literality does not meet the emotional imperative of involvement, because it leaves no space for the self.

Language appears to share its evolutionary origins with music and other forms of art, which cannot be said to have a primarily literal meaning, as discussed for example by Douglas/Willats 1994; Livingstone/Thompson 2006, and Treitler 1997. See also Thompson 2009, p.19f and Cross 2003 and 2007 on the role of music in biocultural evolution. Literality is not the issue, neither in art nor in language.

*****

Variations: No. 5, page 83

Humans are *biological systems*. (See Maturana/Varela 1973; Maturana 1975) Stability can only be maintained by the constant *adjustment* of equilibrium. This is a continuous, ongoing process. Walter B. Cannon referred to this ability of the body to regulate its internal environment as *homeostasis* (1929). He also showed how emotional excitement (which is also a reaction to stimuli *outside* the organism, i.e. fear, rage or pain) leads to bodily (somatic) changes (1934, 1963).

Back-up notes

See also Luhmann 1990, p.271f and 383f, and Maturana 1978, p.36f, 43f and 46f, on how systems maintain their integrity, let in new information and interact with other systems, and Watzlawick et al 1957, p.31 and 134 on homeostatic adjustment in human communication.

See Esther Fischer-Homberger 1996, on the relation between pain, our psychological well-being and the modern separation of the soma and the psyche.

Variations: No. 5, page 84
For a discussion of Galen as a healer of the soul, as well as the body, see for example Maróth 1993, and Fischer-Homberger 1996.

Aristotle was not only a philosopher and rhetorician, but, first and foremost, a biologist, and it was as a biologist that he looked at human interaction. (See for example *De Anima*, p.128f and Hugh Lawson-Tancred's introduction, p.32f)

Being alone is painful. Rejection hurts. Yes, it really does, as is revealed by neuroimaging studies that suggest that 'social pain' has a similar 'neurocognitive function to 'physical pain', and alerts us 'when we have sustained injury to our social connections...' (Eisenberger et al 2003)

Social loss causes pain. Again, the 'emotional pain induced by social exclusion' can be shown by MRI (magnetic resonance imaging). MRI has revealed a 'plethora of neural correlates of affective states', while 'the central cingulated region is known to integrate emotion and cognition'. (Panksepp 2003, p.238)

The body reacts to social isolation because it is dangerous: '... it is not hard to comprehend the strong survival value conferred by common neural pathways that elaborate both social attachment and the affective qualities of physical pain.' (Panksepp 2003, p.238)

See also: Adolphs 2001; Adolphs et al 2003; Andersen/Guerrero 1998a and 1998b; Barbalet 2001; Barbee et al 1998; Brewer 2008; Cacioppo et al 2002; Damasio 1995; Darwin 1872; Forgas/Fitness 2008; Frijda 1994; Lane 2000; Lane et al 2000; Ledoux 2000; Libet 1989; Macdonald/Leary 2005; Mandler 1984; Öhman et al 2000; Parker 1998; Rolls 1999; Scherer 1994; Segrin 1998; Williams 2001; Zadro et al 2008, on how emotional closeness is necessary for our physical well-being.

For an overview of the philosophical debate on the 'Logic of Affect', see Redding 1999.

The ability to feel with another person, otherwise know as empathy, is a product of evolution. Our ability to develop a theory of mind, i.e. to know that other people think differently from us, and to imagine what they might be thinking and feeling, is thought to be closely linked to our language ability. (See, for example, Meltzoff/Decety 2003; Rizollatti et al 2002; Rizzolatti et al 2003)

Variations: No. 5, page 85

Archimedes did not, we assume, simply say, *Ah, mmh, Eureka, I think.* The story goes that he jumped up and cried it out: *Eureka!*

On science, inspiration and creativity see, for example, Arthur Koestler (1964, p.87f and 212f.), as well as on the fine line between art and science when it comes to truth:

> I think I have said enough to show that 'scientific evidence' is a rather elastic term and that 'verification' is always a relative affair. [...] 'The evidence proves' is a statement which is supposed to confer on Science a privileged intimacy with truth which art can never hope to attain. But 'the evidence proves' that the statement in quotes is always based on an act of faith.
>
> Koestler 1964, p.246

Science and art do not happen in separate, hermetically sealed worlds. They are part of the same world, and partake in the same human perception. That is why science and art can be translated into each other, and why science can be translated for non-scientists. It is a question of re-ordering the pieces of the puzzle.

What Alan Sillitoe says of the creative process of writing, applies, *mutatis mutandis*, to any process of communication.

> ... the novel, while mirroring the sort of atmosphere I grew up in, is a work of the imagination in that all the actors in it are put together from jigsaw pieces assembled so that no identifiable characters came out at the end. I imagine novelists of the middle-class condition also perform in this way.

> I had no theme in my head except the joy of writing, the sweat of writing clearly and truthfully, the work of trying to portray ordinary people as I knew them, and in such a way that they would *recognise themselves*. (Emphasis added)
>
> Alan Sillitoe 1974 (1958)
> Introduction to *Saturday Night and Sunday Morning*

Scientific knowledge can also be presented in such a way that it can be recognised by 'ordinary people'. The jigsaw puzzle simply needs to be reassembled. See also Kaiser-Cooke 1999, 2000 and 2004, p.217f as well as Kuhn 1962, p.185f.

C.P. Snow, in his well-known lectures on the incompatibility of art and science, suggests that the two inhabit different cultures and are therefore not mutually understandable (1959). However, the fact that cultures speak different languages has never yet been an obstacle to mutual understanding, i.e. translation.

Thomas Kuhn (1962, p.202-203) and Paul Feyerabend (1984, p.104) also speak of the incommensurability of paradigms, theories and different interpretations of reality. But in the real world of living and communicating human beings, translation has never been a question of commensurability in the sense of complete logical equivalence. Understanding does not require that *everything* be understood. For more detailed discussion of the philosophical implications of this argument, see Kaiser-Cooke 2004, p.185f.

Moreover, as both Kuhn (1962, p.202-204) and Karl Popper (1956, p.156-157) have pointed out, scientists who 'live' in different paradigms can begin to understand each other by learning each other's idiom.

Variations: No. 5, page 86
Kandinsky, writing about the artist's own need (1914, p.35 and p.53), makes it clear that meaning is not the exterior perception, but what is beneath it and gives rise to it:

> In a conversation with an interesting person... we do not bother about the words he uses, nor the spelling of those words, nor the breath necessary for speaking them, nor the movement of his tongue and lips, nor the physiological effect on our nerves. We realise that these things, though interesting and important,

are not the main things of the moment, but that the meaning and idea is what concerns us.
Kandinsky 1914, p.49

We are all artists – and we are all poets.

Living systems are autonomous entities [...]; all the phenomena related to them depend on the way their autonomy is realized [...] this autonomy is the result of their organization as systems in continuous self-production. [...] such systems [are called] *autopoietic systems...*
Maturana 1978, p.36, original emphasis

Autopoiesis comes from the Greek for *self* and *to make, produce, create*. *Poiesis* is also the word behind *poetry*: A poet is a creator. We create our own world, and speak our own worlds. Our truth is always un-speakable. Like all poets, we show it by not saying it.

Variations: No. 5, page 87

Vera Brittain's memories of the First World War are captured in her book *Testament of Youth*.

Understanding too much leaves no room for movement. Two systems in harmony do not experience any perturbation or learning (see Maturana 1978, p.45f). There is no disorder and no need for adjustment. The result is inertia or the 'emptiness of homogeneity'. (Arnheim 1971, p.52)

If a system is so merged with another system that it sees no difference, it can no longer define itself. It cannot see itself, because there is no longer any self to be seen. This also means it cannot see the *other*. Difference must be maintained so that there is space to see where one starts and the other stops (see Maturana 1978, p.31f and 'autopoietic closure', p.37)

Empathy, i.e. seeing things through somebody else's eyes, also requires that we see them as *different*, as *somebody else*. Empathy is not the same as identification.

For a discussion of empathy and self, see Bauer 2005; Binder 1999, p.72f and 83f; Eisenberg/Strayer 1990; Ford/Maher 1998; Frith/Frith 1999; Gallese 2003a and 2003b; Gergely 1994; Gopnik/Meltzoff 1994;

Back-up notes

Mascolo/Fischer 1998; Plutchik 1990; Rizzolatti/Sinigaghia 2008; Rogers 1975; Sternberg/Spear-Swerling 1998; Strayer 1990; Wicker et al 2003; Wispé 1990.

Erich Fromm links understanding to empathy and love:
> The condition of [...] empathy is a crucial facet of the capacity for love. To understand another means to love him [sic] – not in the erotic sense, but in the sense of reaching out to him and of overcoming the fear of losing oneself. Understanding and loving are inseparable. If they are separate, it is a cerebral process and the door to essential understanding remains closed.
> 1994, p.193

We are all born with the capacity to distinguish between ourselves and others in order to be able to see others as other than us, which is an essential condition for any inter-action, and thus for understanding.

Changing our perspective is a biological necessity: We can all adapt to new environments, cultures and languages (unless we decide we don't want to). Even though different cultures see the world in different colours (Deutscher 2010) it does not mean that they are not able to see all the colours of the rainbow.

Variations: No. 5, pages 88-89
It is only when we have space, or distance, that we can change our position in relation to a person or a thing, or in other words, look at them from a different angle. Looking from a different place means seeing things differently. The familiar becomes, to a greater or lesser extent, unfamiliar.

This defamiliarisation, whether in art (see Paskow 2004, p.69), science (Costazza 1993; Koestler 1964, p.93, 212 and 249f; Wallner 1993), or in our everyday relations with fellow human beings, enables us to gain another perspective on the matter *without losing our own*. There need be no question of attaining a neutral vantage point – of course this is impossible – and it is also unnecessary. Perspectival shift is a facet of everyday life (see Higgins 1997 on music and perspectival listening), and not only for humans. Apes can also change their perspective on things. (See for example Mitchell 1994, p.92f)

Changing perspective, in other words, re-ordering experience, is an integral part of the creative process. This is what Bruner refers to as 'the combinatorial acts' that produce effective surprise (1962, p.22). The prerequisite for this reordering of experience is cognitive 'detachment' or a '...willingness to divorce oneself from the obvious'. (Bruner 1962, p.23.) It is clear that obviousness is also relative to our vantage point.

Culture-specific or language-specific perception does not confine us to a cultural straitjacket: Relativism is not absolute. For more detailed discussion of cultural and linguistic relativism, and objective relativity see Kaiser-Cooke 2004, p.157f.

We are not confined to our own perspective, to our own world or to the purely objective. Ludwig Wittgenstein describes and analyses language as a system of logic: 'Die Logik erfüllt die Welt; die Grenzen der Welt sind auch ihre Grenzen.' (Logic fills the world; the limits of the world are also the limits of logic.) [...] 'Was wir nicht denken können, das können wir nicht denken; wir können also auch nicht *sagen*, was wir nicht denken können.' (We cannot think what is un-thinkable; we cannot *say* what we cannot think. Original emphasis. *Tractatus* 5.561, p.67.)

'Dass die Welt *meine* Welt ist, das zeigt sich darin, dass die Grenzen der Sprache (der Sprache, die allein ich verstehe) die Grenzen *meiner* Welt bedeuten.' (That the world is *my* world is shown by the fact that the limits of language (language that I alone understand), signify the limits of *my* world. Original emphasis. *Tractatus* 5.62, p.67)

'Die Welt und das Leben sind eins.' (The world and life are one. *Tractatus* 5.621, p.67)

Even if we are talking about private language and private worlds, this cannot be the case, for at least two reasons:

Mathematical logic does not rule the world. Living beings – which of course includes human beings – are plastic adaptable systems which, far from functioning according to formal logic and equations, adapt to the contingencies of life, which are unforeseeable and unpredictable, but nevertheless probable in the respective system's environment. It is this malleability or plasticity which maintains life, and systemic integrity. The limits of logic cannot be the limits of the world, otherwise it would come to a standstill.

Back-up notes

The limits of my language cannot be contiguous with the limits of my world, because what I say goes out to become part of somebody else's world. Interaction is the point of the exercise. We do not speak what we think. To say that we do presupposes conscious evaluation of our utterances and equivalence between thought and speech, as well as between emotion and speech (see Zajonc 1994 on unconscious emotions). It also presupposes, of course, that the purpose of language is to produce true statements or propositions and that to understand means to understand *propositions*. ('Der Satz ist ein Bild der Wirklichkeit.' The statement is an image of reality. *Tractatus* 4.01., p.26.)

'Einen Satz verstehen, heißt, wissen, was der Fall ist, wenn er wahr ist.' (To understand a statement means to know what is, if the statement is true. *Tractatus* 4.024, p.28.)

But it is precisely when we try to understand statements, rather than the people who are uttering them, that we fail to understand, i.e. to grasp *meaning*.

Similarly, translating does not mean, as Wittgenstein suggests, that we translate parts or components of statements ('Die Übersetzung einer Sprache in eine andere geht nicht so vor sich, dass man jeden *Satz* der einen in einen *Satz* der anderen übersetzt, sondern nur die Satzbestandteile werden übersetzt.' *Tractatus* 4.025, p.28)

The truth of what we say does not depend on the words we speak. Language may denote objects or even sensations (see Kripke 1982, p.14f), but this is not what words or statements mean. We do not denote, i.e. talk *about* our sensations or emotions. All language is 'sensation' in that it reveals our inner meaning. It does this obliquely. We don't have to ask ourselves whether 'the grass is really green'. (See Kripke 1982, p.20) We don't mean facts in the sense of verifiable empirical data. We mean ourselves. There can therefore be no such thing as a 'senseless' or 'meaningless' statement.

Language isn't about the truth content of propositions. It doesn't matter whether the grass *really* is green. Language isn't about mathematical logic, equations or equivalence. It's about us: It is our attempt to share, yes, the world we construct and privately inhabit, but through the faulty, imprecise perturbations of our living, plastic, irritated and irritable flesh-and-blood systems. There is not even a one-to-one match between our emotional logic and the sentences we utter. Words are just the surface symptoms of internal perturbation.

We don't *tell* the truth, we show it. Jean-Jacques Rousseau laments his inability to always be truthful '... il fallait avoir le courage et la force d'être vrai toujours' (4ième Promenade, p.91), but recognises the difference between the Truth and his own truthfulness ('vérité' and 'véracité', 4ième Promenade, p.82-83). We cannot but be truthful, for those who care to look beyond word truth or propositional truth. These are sterile truths (see also Rousseau on 'vérités stériles', 4ième Promenade, p.78) – they are divorced from the complex life experience which gives rise to them.

In Brian Friel's play *Translations*, people understand each other's truth again and again, though they do not speak the same language. Maire, an Irish woman, and Yolland, and English soldier, show each other their love in Irish and English, though they speak 'meaningless' sentences. The words are almost irrelevant. Words are simply the medium for what they feel. Maire and Yolland don't translate each other's words. They translate their feelings. It is their internal states that match, and are true, not the mere surface ripples that these states produce.

For all the variations which it can assume, there is only one human reality. Our private worlds are only private in a collective context; their privacy does not exclude their being part of one bigger world.

Meaningful language, like meaningful art, must be based on the assumption of a fundamental unity. And we all have '... the desire to immerse ourselves within the felicity of an all-inclusive unity.' (Mark Rothko 2004, p.37) Art which leaves out individual humanity can never be universal; it is merely archetypical (like Fascist art) and cannot move us. See also Mark Rothko 2004, p.22f on the relation between the particular and the universal in art.

*****

Variations: No. 6, page 91
Emotions are a biological necessity. They tell us what we need, and what we don't need. They are not separate from thinking, or cognition, but are part of it. See, for example, Averill 1994; Batson et al 1990; Clore 1994a, 1994b and 1994c; Clore et al 2000; Cooper 1999; Damasio 1994; Ekman 1998a and 1998b; Ellis 1996; Krumhansl 2002; Levenson 1994; Planalp

Back-up notes

1998; Prainsack 2000 and 2004. And Daniel Goleman's seminal work, *Emotional Intelligence* (1995), shows that emotion *is* cognition.

'Nursing, vocalization and play all share a common motivation for social interaction.' (Insel 2003, p.351) Social stimuli appear to be linked to a 'reward pathway'. (Insel 2003, p.351) mediating the release of the neuropeptides oxytocin and vasopressin. (Insel 2003, p.356) Social interaction brings neurobiological rewards. The 'neurobiology of attachment' can be regarded as fundamental for the 'transition from reptiles to mammals'. (Insel 2003, p.351; see also Maclean 1990, cited in Insel 2003.)

We are all 'stoned': We all need interaction with others to know who we are. Social attachment is 'addictive' (Insel 2003). See also Kosfeld et al 2005.

Emotional experience is stored in our physical bodies. It is somatic. We really do know it 'in our bones'. See also Joachim Bauer's discussion of somatic memory (2002).

For an overview of what emotions or feelings 'really are' see Griffiths 1997; Panksepp 1994; Terada 2001 and Turner 2007.

Facts are things that happen. The word fact derives from the latin *facere*, to do or make, an action, a thing done, something that has actual existence. *Fact: an occurrence, quality, or relation, the reality of which is manifest in experience or maybe inferred with certainty. Something that makes a statement or a proposition true or false; that hinges on the actual evidence.* (Webster's Third New International Dictionary, 1961.) Emotions happen.

What is a law of nature? What we call a law of nature is a regularity: It is not an immutable rule. This means that, according to how the world is, certain occurrences will happen. However, it does *not* mean that all these occurrences will be exactly the same, nor does it mean that they are entirely predictable.

As Schrödinger points out in his well-known essay (1922), complete predictability is not possible. What we see, measure, observe, is not a complete picture of 'Nature', but an incomplete human interpretation of what we can perceive (p.24-25). The 'laws' that we formulate don't refer to the actual individual occurrences, but to a prototypical case, which never happens in reality (p.13f). Just as anatomy books show a prototypical body which we never meet in real life, the 'laws of nature' give us something to go on, indicate what to expect, so that when it really happens, we can recognise it – and know where to look to detect the deviations from the prototype.

Certainty and precision are not features of the real world. Not even in the natural sciences. What is important is to be aware of the uncertainty and the imprecision (p.25). Schrödinger emphasises that it is necessary to relinquish the idea of a purely objective description of Nature ('Den notgedrungenen Verzicht auf eine rein objektive Beschreibung der Natur...', p.26). Even the 'exact' sciences are not exact. The more 'exact' they are, the more the lack of exactitude becomes evident.

Variations: No. 6, page 92

We cannot not communicate (Watzlawick et al 1967, p.48-49) because not to communicate means not to survive.

Since communication always involves irritation, or perturbation, we actively need to thrash out what we mean, or to agree that we disagree. Negotiation of reference is the reason why we go to all the bother. (Kress 1989, p.12f, 32f and 79f) Reference might well be inscrutable, but for the purposes of real-life communication, it doesn't matter: The difference is what keeps the whole thing going.

Moreover, understanding everything can never be a realistic communicative goal, because of our biological constitution. Equivalence is not humanly possible. And it is not necessary. Given that equivalence is not an issue, the discussion of the 'impossibility' and 'indeterminacy' of translation (Quine 1960, 1969) becomes irrelevant. Communication is always 'indeterminate'.

*****

Variations: No. 7, page 97

René Descartes: 'Je pense, donc je suis.' (I think, therefore I am.) In *Discours de la méthode* (1637/1966, p.60).

Blaise Pascal:
> Le cœur a ses raisons que la raison ne connaît point; On le sait en mille choses [...] est-ce par raison que vous vous aimez?
> *Pensées*, Section IV, §277

[The heart has its reasons, which reason does not know. We know this through a hundred different things... ... is it reason that makes you love yourself?]

> Deux excès: exclure la raison, n'admettre que la raison.
> *Pensées*, Section IV, §253

[Two extremes: excluding reason, and using only reason.]

Variations: No. 7, page 98
Science requires '... open-mindedness [...] a willingness to construe knowledge and values from multiple perspectives without loss of commitment to one's values.' (Bruner 1990, p.30)

Variations: No. 7, page 99
Equilibrium, or perfect order, is a final state which stops 'the stream of life'. (Arnheim 1971, p.56)

Variations: No. 7, page 100
We are all translators. As indeed pointed out by Zygmunt Bauman. (1999, p.xlvii)

Our realities meet, we understand other people's worlds indirectly through the words they use. We understand the expression of their reality by looking behind, between and beyond their words. We can look at our world through their eyes, and at theirs through ours. We do not have to leave ourselves to look at someone else. This is why we are able to communicate, to share our experience. We can say things in other words because we can see beyond our own.

We are all translators but, as explained elsewhere (Kaiser-Cooke 2004, 2007), I do not mean that professional translators only do what everyone else does. Yes, 'anyone' can become a professional translator, because the ability to translate – change perspective, detach meaning from form, re-structure the order that we are used to seeing – is something that all humans are endowed with. If they weren't, no amount of training in the world could make us learn how to do it.

Of course, it takes years of training for people to do systematically, consciously and professionally, what all people can do intuitively. Just like professional singers, runners or poets, professional translators develop abilities and cognitive potential that all human beings share by virtue of being human. None of us can do anything that is not humanly possible.

*****

Finale, page 107

Flaubert's text in French:

Ainsi leur rencontre avait eu l'importance d'une aventure. Ils s'étaient, tout de suite, accrochés par des fibres secrètes. D'ailleurs, comment expliquer les sympathies? Pourquoi telle particularité, telle imperfection, indifférente ou odieuse dans celui-ci, enchante-t-elle dans celui-là? Ce qu'on appelle le coup de foudre est vrai pour toutes les passions.

Gustave Flaubert, *Bouvard et Pécuchet*
Paris: Garnier-Flammarion (1966)
Unfinished, begun in 1874, p.38

Emotional evidence

Music
Beethoven, Ludwig van. *Symphony No. 9*, D minor
Chopin, Frédéric. *Prélude B minor Op.28 No. 6*
Chopin, Frédéric. *Prélude C sharp minor Op.28 No. 8*
Chopin, Frédéric. *Prélude D flat Major Op.28 No. 15*
Dvořák, Antonín. *Rusalka*
Moustaki, Georges. *Ma Solitude*

Painting, photography and painters
Birtukaine. *My Home*. In: Children's Calendar, January, Light for the World (2011)
Cooke, Molly / Cooke, Sadie. *Life: Rebecca, Lilly, Hannah and Molly Cooke*
Eisner, Will. 1985. *Comics & sequential art*
Kandinsky, Wassily. *Concerning the spiritual in art* (Über das Geistige in der Kunst, translation by M.T.H. Sadler)
Manet, Eduard. *Une botte d'asperges (Bunch of Asparagus)*
Matisse, Henri. Quoted in Barr, Alfred. *Matisse – His Art and his Public*
Ritt, Jakob. 2011. *Darling Ducks*
Ritt, Jakob. 2011. *Stoned*
Rothko, Mark. 2004. *The artist's reality*
Van Gogh,Vincent. *A Pair of Shoes* (1886)

Novels, stories and plays
Albom, Mitch. *the five people you meet in Heaven*
Brittain, Vera. *Testament of Youth*
Eliot, George. *Middlemarch*
Flaubert, Gustav. *Bouvard et Pécuchet*
Forster, E.M. *The Prince's Tale and Other Uncollected Writings*
Friel, Brian. *Translations*
Gaskell, Elizabeth. *North and South*
Milne, A.A. *The House at Pooh Corner*
Saint-Exupéry, Antoine de. *Le Petit Prince*
Sartre, Jean-Paul. *Huis Clos*
Sand, George. *Histoire de ma vie*, vol. XIII, Paris (1855)
Sillitoe, Alan. *Saturday night and Sunday morning*
Wharton, Edith. *The Age of Innocence*

Philosophy
Aristotle. *The Art of Rhetoric*. (Translation by Hugh Lawson-Tancred)
Aristotle. *Poetics*. (Translation by Malcolm Heath)
Aristotle. *De Anima (On the soul)*. (Translation by Hugh Lawson-Tancred)
Descartes, René. *Discours de la méthode*
Heidegger, Martin. 1926 (2006). *Sein und Zeit.*
Heidegger, Martin. 1936 (1960). *Der Ursprung des Kunstwerkes.*

Heidegger, Martin. 2002. The Essence of Truth. (Translation by Ted Sadler. Original Title: *Vom Wesen der Wahrheit*. 1945)
Heidegger, Martin. 1971. *Poetry, Language, Thought*. (Translation by Albert Hochstadter)
Pascal, Blaise. *Pensées et Opuscules*
Rousseau, Jean-Jacques. *Les rêveries du promeneur solitaire*

Poetry
Aragon, Louis. *Les Poètes*
Aragon, Louis. *J'entends, j'entends*
Auden, W.H. *September 1, 1939*
Keats, John. *La belle dame sans merci*
Rilke, Rainer-Maria. *Book of hours. Love Poems to God.* (*Das Stundenbuch*. Translation by Anita Barrows, and Joanna Macy)
Wordsworth, William. *On Seeing Some Tourists*
Wordsworth, William. *My Heart leaps up when I behold*
Wordsworth, William. *I wandered lonely as a cloud*

Letters
Rilke, Rainer Maria. *Briefe an einen jungen Dichter*

Miscellaneous
Your life

Translations of foreign-language texts by Michèle Cooke, unless otherwise stated.

Scientific evidence

Adolphs, Ralph. 2001. *The neurobiology of social cognition.* In: *Current opinion in Neurobiology* 11, 231-239

Adolphs, Ralph/Tranel, D./Damasio, Antonio. 2003. *Dissociable neural systems for recognizing emotions.* In: *Brain Cognition* 52, 61-69

Ames-Lewis, Francis. 2000. *The Intellectual Life of the Early Renaissance Artist.* New Haven: Yale University Press

Andersen, Peter A./Guerrero, Laura K. (Eds.). 1998. *Handbook of Communication and Emotion. Research, Theory, Applications and Contexts.* San Diego: Academic Press

Andersen, Peter A./Guerrero, Laura K. 1998a. *Principles of Communication and Emotion in Social Interaction.* In: Andersen, Peter A./Guerrero, Laura K. (Eds.). 1998. *Handbook of Communication and Emotion. Research, Theory, Applications and Contexts,* 49-96. San Diego: Academic Press

Andersen, Peter A./Guerrero, Laura K. 1998b. *The Bright Side of Relational Communication: Interpersonal Warmth as a Social Emotion.* In: Andersen, Peter A./Guerrero, Laura K. (Eds.). 1998. *Handbook of Communication and Emotion. Research, Theory, Applications and Contexts,* 303-329. San Diego: Academic Press

Aristotle. *De Anima (On the soul).* Translation by Lawson-Tancred, Hugh. 1986. London: Penguin

Aristotle. *The Art of Rhetoric.* Translation by Lawson-Tancred, Hugh. 1991. London: Penguin

Aristotle. *Poetics.* Translation by Heath, Malcolm. 1996. London: Penguin

Arnheim, Rudolf. 1971. *Entropy and Art. An Essay on Disorder and Order.* Berkeley/Los Angeles/London: University of California Press

Averill, James R. 1994. *I Feel, Therefore I Am – I Think.* In: Ekman, Paul/Davidson, R.J. (Eds.). 1994. *The nature of Emotion. Fundamental questions,* 379-385. Oxford/New York: Oxford University Press

Baker, Myron/Cunningham, Michael. 1985. *The Biology of Bird-Song Dialects.* In: *Behavioral and Brain Sciences,* 85-88. Cambridge: Cambridge University Press

Barbalet, Jack M. 2001. *Emotion, social theory, and social structure.* Cambridge: Cambridge University Press

Barbee, Anita P./Rowatt, Tammy L./Cunningham, Michael R. 1998. *When a Friend Is in Need: Feelings about Seeking, Giving, and Receiving Social Support.* In: Andersen, Peter A./Guerrero, Laura K. (Eds.). 1998. *Handbook of Communication and Emotion. Research, Theory, Applications and Contexts,* 281-301. San Diego: Academic Press

Barr, Alfred H. Jr. 1951. *Matisse – His Art and his Public.* New York: Museum of Modern Art

Batson, Daniel C./Fultz, Jim/Schoenrade, Patricia A. 1990. *Adults' emotional reactions to the distress of others.* In: Eisenberg, Nancy/Strayer, Janet (Eds.). 1990. *Empathy and its Development,* 163-184. Cambridge: Cambridge University Press

Bauer, Joachim. 2002 (2007). *Das Gedächtnis des Körpers – Wie Beziehungen und Lebensstile unsere Gene steuern*. Munich: Piper
Bauer, Joachim. 2005 (2006). *Warum ich fühle, was du fühlst*. Munich: Wilhelm Heyne
Berlyne, D.E. 1971. *Aesthetics and psychobiology*. New York: Appleton Century Crofts
Binder, Ute. 1999. *Empathieentwicklung und Pathogenese in der klientenzentrierten Psychotherapie – Überlegungen zu einem systemimmanenten Konzept*. Eschborn/Frankfurt am Main: Dietmar Klotz
Brewer, Marilyn B. 2008. *Social Identity and Close Relationships*. In: Forgas, Joseph P./Fitness, Julie (Eds.). 2008. *Social Relationships. Cognitive, Affective, and Motivational Processes*, 167-184. New York: Psychology Press
Bruner, Jerome. 1962. *On Knowing – Essays for the Left Hand*. Cambridge, MA/London: Harvard University Press
Bruner, Jerome. 1990. *Acts of meaning*. Cambridge, MA/London: Harvard University Press
Byrne, Richard. 1995. *The Thinking Ape*. Oxford/New York: Oxford University Press
Cacioppo, John T./Hawkley, Luise C./Crawford, Elizabeth L./Ernst, John/Burleson, Mary H./Kowalewski, Ray B./Malarkey, William B./Van Cauther, Eve/Bernston, Gary G. 2002. *Loneliness and Health: Potential Mechanisms*. In: *Psychosomatic Medicine* 64, 407-417
Cannon, Walter B. 1929. *Organization for Physiological Homeostasis*. In: *Physiological Review* 9, 399-341
Cannon, Walter B. 1934. *Bodily changes in pain, hunger, fear and rage. An account of recent researches into the function of emotional excitement*. New York/London: Appleton-Century
Cannon, Walter B. 1963. *The Wisdom of the Body*. New York: Norton
Cheney, Dorothy L./Seyforth, Robert M. 1990. *How Monkeys See the World*. Chicago/London: University of Chicago Press
Chomsky, Noam. 1993. *Language and Thought*. Wakefield, Rhode Island/London: Moyer Bell
Clore, Gerald L. 1994a. *Why Emotions Require Cognition*. In: Ekman, Paul/Davidson, R.J. (Eds.). 1994a. *The Nature of Emotion. Fundamental Questions*, 181-191. Oxford/New York: Oxford University Press
Clore, Gerald L. 1994b. *Why Emotions are Felt*. In: Ekman, Paul/Davidson, R.J. (Eds.). 1994b. *The Nature of Emotion. Fundamental Questions*, 103-111. Oxford/New York: Oxford University Press
Clore, Gerald L. 1994c. *Why emotions are never unconscious*. In: Ekman, Paul/Davidson, R.J. (Eds.). 1994c. *The Nature of Emotion. Fundamental Questions*, 285-290. Oxford/New York: Oxford University Press
Clore, Gerald L./Ortony, Andrew. 2000. *Cognition in Emotion: Always, Sometimes, or Never?* In: Lane, Richard D./Nadel, Lynn (Eds.). 2000. *Cognitive Neuroscience of Emotion*, 24-61. Oxford/New York: Oxford University Press
Cooper, John M. 1999. *Reason and Emotion*. Princeton: Princeton University Press
Costazza, Markus. 1993. *Drei methodische Zugänge zur Interdisziplinarität und das Konzept der Verfremdung*. In: Wallner, Fritz G./Schwimmer, Josef/Costazza,

Markus (Eds.). 1993. *Grenzziehungen zum Konstruktiven Realismus*, 52-67. Vienna: WUV – Universitätsverlag
Cross, Ian. 2003. Music and biocultural evolution. In: Clayton, Martin/Herbert, Trevor/Middleton Richard (Eds.). 2003a. *The cultural study of music: A critical introduction*, 19-30. London/New York: Routledge
Cross, Ian. 2007. Music and cognitive evolution. In: Dunbar, Robin/Barrett, Louise (Eds.). 2007. *OUP Handbook of Evolutionary Psychology*, 649-667. Oxford/New York: Oxford University Press
Damasio, Antonio. 1994 (2006). *Descartes' Error*. London: Vintage
Damasio, Antonio. 1995. *The Feeling of What Happens. Body and Emotion in the Making of Consciousness*. New York: Harcourt Brace & Company
Darwin, Charles. 1872 (1998). *The Expression of the Emotions in Man and Animals*. London: Fontana Press
Davies, Stephen. 1997. Why listen to sad music if it makes one feel sad? In: Robinson, Jenefer (Ed.). 1997. *Music and Meaning*, 242-253. Ithaca/London: Cornell University Press
Derrida, Jacques. 1989. Restitutions of the Truth in Pointing (Pointure). In: Preziosi, Donald (Ed.). 1998. *The Art of Art History: a critical anthology*, 427-449. Oxford/New York: Oxford University Press
Descartes, René. 1637 (1966). *Discours de la méthode*. Paris: Flammarion
Deutscher, Guy. 2010. *Through the Language Glass. How Words Colour Your World*. London: William Heinemann
Dissanayake, Ellen. 2000. Antecedents of the temporal arts in early mother-infant interactions. In: Wallin, Nils L./Merker Björn/Brown Steven (Eds.). 2000. *The Origins of Music*, 388-410. Cambridge, MA: MIT Press
Douglas, Sheila/Willatts, Peter. 1994. The relationship between musical ability and literacy skills. In: *Journal of Research in Reading* 17(2), 99-107
Dunbar, Robin I.M./Spoors, M. 1995. Social Networks, support cliques and kinship. In: *Human Nature* 6, 273-290
Dunbar, Robin. 1996. *Grooming, Gossip and the Evolution of Language*. London: Faber&Faber
Eisenberg, Nancy/Strayer Janet. 1990. Critical issues in the study of empathy. In: Eisenberg, Nancy/Strayer, Janet (Eds.). 1990. *Empathy and its Development*, 3-16. Cambridge: Cambridge University Press
Eisenberg, Nancy/Strayer, Janet (Eds.). 1990. *Empathy and its Development*. Cambridge: Cambridge University Press
Eisenberger, Naomi/Lieberman, Matthew D./Williams, Kipling D. 2003. Does rejection hurt? An fMRI study of social exclusion. In: *Science* 302, 290-292
Eisner, Will. 1985 (2008). *Comics & sequential art*. New York/London: W.W. Norton&Company
Ekman, Paul/Davidson, Richard J. (Eds.). 1994. *The Nature of Emotion. Fundamental Questions*. Oxford/New York: Oxford University Press
Ekman, Paul. 1998a. Afterword. In: Darwin, Charles. 1872. *The expression of the emotions in man and animals*, 363-394. London: Fontana Press
Ekman, Paul. 1998b. Preface to the Third Edition. In: Darwin, Charles. 1872. *The expression of the emotions in man and animals*, xiii-xix. London: Fontana Press

Ellis, Ralph. 1996. *Questioning Consciousness: The Interplay of Imagery, Cognition and Emotion in the Human Brain*. Amsterdam: Benjamins
Fairclough, Norman. 1989. *Language and power*. New York: Longman
Farías, Victor. 1989. *Heidegger und der Nationalsozialismus*. Frankfurt am Main: S. Fischer (Translations from French and Spanish by Klaus Laermann, original title: *Heidegger et le nazisme*. 1987. Lagrasse: Editions Verdier. English translation: *Heidegger and Nazism* by Gabriel R. Ricci.)
Feldman, Jerome A. 2006 (2008). *From Molecule to Metaphor. A Neural Theory of Language*. Cambridge, MA: MIT Press
Ferrari, Michel/Sternberg, Robert J. (Eds.). 1998. *Self Awareness. Its Nature and Development*. New York: Guilford Press
Feyerabend, Paul. 1978. *Der wissenschaftstheoretische Realismus und die Autorität der Wissenschaften. Ausgewählte Schriften, Vol.1*. Braunschweig/Wiesbaden: Friedrich Viehweg & Sohn
Feyerabend, Paul. 1984. *Wissenschaft als Kunst*. Frankfurt am Main: Suhrkamp
Fichte, Johann Gottlieb. 1794 (1997). *Grundlage der gesamten Wissenschaftslehre*. Hamburg: Felix Meiner
Fischer-Homberger, Esther. 1996. *Zum klassisch-neuzeitlichen Umgang mit dem Schmerz: Die Schmerz-Bekämpfung und ihr Preis*. In: Barta, Heinz/Grabner-Niel, Elisabeth (Eds.). 1996. *Wissenschaft und Verantwortlichkeit*, 290-320. Innsbruck: Universitätsverlag
Fonagy, Peter. 2001. *The human genome and the representational world: the role of early mother-infant interaction in creating an interpersonal interpretative mechanism*. In: *Bulletin of the Menninger Clinic* 65, 427-448
Ford, Martin E./Maher, Michelle A. 1998. *Self-Awareness and Social Intelligence: Web Pages, Search Engines, and Navigational Control*. In: Ferrari, Michel/Sternberg, Robert J. (Eds.). 1998. *Self Awareness. Its Nature and Development*, 191-218. New York: Guilford Press
Forgas, Joseph P./Fitness, Julie. 2008. *Evolutionary, Sociocultural, and Intrapsychic Influences on Personal Relationships: An Introductory Review*. In: Forgas, Joseph P./Fitness, Julie (Eds.). 2008. *Social Relationships. Cognitive, Affective, and Motivational Processes*, 3-20. New York: Psychology Press
Forgas, Joseph P./Fitness, Julie (Eds.). 2008. *Social Relationships. Cognitive, Affective, and Motivational Processes*. New York: Psychology Press
Frijda, Nico H. 1994. *Emotions Are Functional, Most of the Time*. In: Ekman, Paul/Davidson, R.J. (Eds.). 1994. *The Nature of Emotion. Fundamental Questions*, 112-122. Oxford/New York: Oxford University Press
Frith, Chris D./Frith, Uta. 1999. *Interacting minds – a biological basis*. In: *Science* 26, 1692-1695
Fromm, Erich. 1994 (2005). *The Art of Listening*. New York: Continuum International
Gallese, Vittorio. 2003a. *The roots of empathy: The shared manifold hypothesis and the neural basis of intersubjectivity*. In: *Psychopathology* 36, 171-180
Gallese, Vittorio. 2003b. *The manifold nature of interpersonal relations: the quest for a common mechanism*. In: *Philosophical Transactions of The Royal Society, London* B 358, 517-528

Geissmann, Thomas. 2000. *Gibbon songs and human music from an evolutionary perspective.* In: Wallin, Nils L./Merker, Björn/Brown, Steven (Eds.). 2000. *The Origins of Music,* 103-123. Cambridge, MA: MIT Press

Gergely, György. 1994. *From self-recognition to theory of mind.* In: Parker, Sue Taylor/Mitchell, Robert W./Boccia, Maria L. (Eds.). 1994. *Self-awareness in animals and humans. Developmental perspectives,* 51-60. Cambridge: University Press

Goleman, Daniel. 1995. *Emotional Intelligence. Why it can matter more than IQ.* New York: Bantam Books

Gómez, Juan-Carlos. 1994. *Mutual awareness in primate communication: A Gricean approach.* In: Parker, Sue Taylor/Mitchell, Robert W./Boccia, Maria L. (Eds.). 1994. *Self-awareness in animals and humans. Developmental perspectives,* 61-80. Cambridge: University Press

Gopnik, Alison/Meltzoff, Andrew N. 1994. *Minds, bodies and persons: Young children's understanding of the self and others as reflected in imitation and theory of mind research.* In: Parker, Sue Taylor/Mitchell, Robert W./Boccia, Maria L. (Eds.). 1994. *Self-awareness in animals and humans. Developmental perspectives,* 166-185. Cambridge: University Press

Griffiths, Paul E. 1997. *What Emotions Really Are. The Problem of Psychological Categories.* Chicago/London: University of Chicago Press

Habermas, Jürgen. 1989. *Vorwort: Heidegger – Werk und Weltanschauung.* In: Farías, Victor. 1989. *Heidegger und der Nationalsozialismus,* 11-37. Frankfurt am Main: S. Fischer (Translations from French and Spanish by Klaus Laermann, original title: *Heidegger et le nazisme.* 1987. Lagrasse: Editions Verdier. English translation: *Heidegger and Nazism* by Gabriel R. Ricci.)

Hawkes, Kristen. 2003. *Grandmothers and the evolution of longevity.* In: *American Journal of Human Biology* 15, 380-400

Hawkes, Kristen. 2004. *Human longevity. The grandmother effect.* In: *Nature* 428, 128-129

Heath, Malcolm. 1996. *Introduction.* In: Aristotle. *Poetics,* vii-lxxiii. Translation by Heath, Malcolm. 1996. London: Penguin

Heidegger, Martin. 1926 (2006). *Sein und Zeit.* Tübingen: Max Niemeyer

Heidegger, Martin. 1936 (1960). *Der Ursprung des Kunstwerkes.* Stuttgart: Reclam

Heidegger, Martin. 2002. *The Essence of Truth.* (Translation by Ted Sadler. Original Title: *Vom Wesen der Wahrheit.* 1945 (1997). Frankfurt am Main: Vittorio Klostermann

Heidegger, Martin. 1971. *Poetry, Language, Thought.* (Translation by Albert Hochstadter) New York: HarperCollins

Heiser, Marc/Iacoboni, Marco/Maeda, Fumiko/Marcus, Jake/Mazziotta, John C. 2003. *The essential role of Broca's area in imitation.* In: *European Journal of Neuroscience* 17, 1123-1128

Higgins, Kathleen Marie. 1997. *Musical Idiosyncrasy and Perspectival Listening.* In: Robinson, Jenefer (Ed.). 1997. *Music and Meaning,* 83-102. Ithaca/London: Cornell University Press

Insel, Thomas. 2003. *Is social attachment an addictive disorder?* In: *Physiology and Behavior* 79, 351-357

Izard, Carroll E. 1977. *Human Emotions.* New York: Plenum Press

Kaindl, Klaus. 1995. *Die Oper als Textgestalt. Perspektiven einer interdisziplinären Übersetzungswissenschaft.* Tübingen: Stauffenburg
Kaiser-Cooke, Michèle. 1999. *Translation and trans-disciplinarity: The Missing Link.* In: *Special Issue of Linguistica Antverpiensa*, 31-37. no. XXXIII
Kaiser-Cooke, Michèle. 2000. *Theory in practice; translation as trans-disciplinary action.* In: Kadric, Mira/Kaindll, Klaus/Pöchhacker, Franz (Eds.). 2000. *Translationswissenschaft. Festschrift für Mary Snell-Hornby zum 60.Geburtstag*, 67-79. Tübingen: Stauffenburg
Kaiser-Cooke, Michèle. 2004. *The Missing Link. Evolution, Reality and the Translation Paradigm.* Frankfurt am Main: Peter Lang
Kaiser-Cooke, Michèle. 2007. *Wissenschaft – Translation – Kommunikation.* Wien: Facultas
Kallberg, Jeffrey. 1996. *Chopin at the Boundaries. Sex, History, and Musical Genre.* Cambridge, MA/London: Harvard University Press
Kandinsky, Wassily. 1914 (1977). *Concerning the Spiritual in Art (Über das geistige in der Kunst.* 1911. English translation and introduction by Sadler, Michael T.H.) New York: Dover
Knorr-Cetina, Karin. 1984. *Die Fabrikation von Erkenntnis. Zur Anthropologie der Naturwissenschaft.* Frankfurt am Main: Suhrkamp
Knorr-Cetina, Karin. 1999. *Epistemic Cultures. How the Sciences Make Knowledge.* Cambridge, MA: Harvard University Press
Koestler, Arthur. 1964 (1981). *The Act of Creation.* London: Picador
Kosfeld, Michael/Heinrichs, Markus/Zak, Paul J./Fischbacher, Urs/Fehr, Ernst. 2005. *Oxytocin increases trust in humans.* In: *Nature* 435, 673
Kress, Gunther. 1989. *Linguistic Processes in Sociocultural Practice.* Oxford/New York: Oxford University Press
Kripke, Saul A. 1982 (1985). *Wittgenstein on Rules and Private Language* . Oxford: Basil Blackwell
Kroodsma, Donald. 2005. *The Singing Life of Birds: The Art and Science of Listening to Birdsong.* New York: Houghton Mifflin Harcourt
Krumhansl, Carol L. 2002. *Music: A link between cognition and emotion.* In: *Current Directions in Psychological Science* 11, 45-50
Kuhn, Thomas. 1962. *The Structure of Scientific Revolutions.* Chicago/London: University of Chicago Press
Lakoff, George. 1980. *The metaphorical structure of the human conceptual system.* In: *Cognitive Science* 4, 195-208
Lakoff, George. 1982. *Categories and cognitive models.* Trier: LAUT
Lakoff, George. 1986. *Two Metaphorical Issues: (1) The Meanings of* Literal, *(2) A Figure of Thought.* Cognitive Science Program, Institute of Cognitive Studies, University of California at Berkeley
Lakoff, George. 1987. *Women, Fire and Dangerous Things. What Categories Reveal about the Mind.* Chicago/London: University of Chicago Press
Lakoff, George/Johnson, Mark. 1980. *Metaphors We Live By.* Chicago/London: University of Chicago Press
Lane, Richard D./Nadel, Lynn (Eds.). 2000. *Cognitive Neuroscience of Emotion.* Oxford/New York: Oxford University Press

Lane, Richard D. 2000. *Neural Correlates of Conscious Emotional Experience*. In: Lane, Richard D./Nadel, Lynn (Eds.). 2000. *Cognitive Neuroscience of Emotion*, 345-370. Oxford/New York: Oxford University Press

Lane, Richard D./Nadel, Lynn/Allen, John J.B./Kaszniak, Alfred W. 2000. *The Study of Emotion from the Perspective of Cognitive Neuroscience*. In: Lane, Richard D./Nadel, Lynn (Eds.). 2000. *Cognitive Neuroscience of Emotion*, 3-12. Oxford/New York: Oxford University Press

Lawson-Tancred, Hugh. 1986. *Introduction*. In: Aristotle. *The Art of Rhetoric*, 11-122. (Translation by Lawson-Tancred, H.C. 1991.) London: Penguin

Ledoux, Joseph. 2000. *Cognitive-Emotional Interactions: Listen to the Brain*. In: Lane, Richard D./Nadel, Lynn (Eds.). 2000. *Cognitive Neuroscience of Emotion*, 129-155. Oxford/New York: Oxford University Press

Levenson, Robert W. 1994. *Human Emotions: A Functional View*. In: Ekman, Paul/Davidson, R.J. (Eds.). 1994. *The Nature of Emotion. Fundamental Questions*, 123-126. Oxford/New York: Oxford University Press

Levinson, Jerrold. 1997. *Music and Negative Emotion*. In: Robinson, Jenefer (Ed.). 1997. *Music and Meaning*, 215-241. Ithaca/London: Cornell University Press

Libet, Benjamin. 1989. *Conscious subjective experience vs. unconscious mental functions: A theory of the cerebral processes involved*. In: Cotterill, Rodney M.J. 1989. *Models of brain function*, 35-49. Cambridge: Cambridge University Press

Livingstone, Steven Robert/Thompson, William Forde. 2006. *Multimodal affective interaction: A comment on musical origins*. In: *Music Perception* 24(1), 89-94

Luhmann, Niklas. 1990. *Die Wissenschaft der Gesellschaft*. Frankfurt am Main: Suhrkamp

Luther, David/Baptista, Luis. 2010. *Urban noise and the cultural evolution of bird songs*. In: *The Proceedings of the Royal Society of Biological Sciences*, 469-473. London: Royal Society Publishing

MacDonald, Geoff/Leary, Mark R. 2005. *Why does social exclusion hurt? The relationship between social and physical pain*. In: *Psychological Bulletin* 131, 202

Maclean, Paul. 1990. *The triune brain in evolution: role in paleocerebral functions*. New York: Plenum

Mandler, George. 1984. *Mind and body: Psychology of emotion and stress*. New York: Norton

Maróth, Miklós. 1993. *Galen als Seelenheiler*. In: Kollesch, Jutta/Nickel, Diethard (Eds.). 1993. *Galen und das hellenistische Erbe. Verhandlungen des IV. Internationalen Galen-Symposiums, 18.-20. September 1998*, 145-155. Stuttgart: Franz Steiner

Mascolo, Michael F./Fischer, Kurt W. 1998. *The Development of Self through the Coordination of Component Systems*. In: Ferrari, Michel/Sternberg, Robert J. (Eds.). 1998. *Self Awareness. Its Nature and Development*, 332-386. New York: Guilford Press

Maturana, Humberto R./ Varela, Francesco. 1973. *De maquinas y seres vivos*. Santiago: Editorial Universitaria Santiago

Maturana, Humberto R. 1975. *The organization of the living: A theory of the living organization*. In: *The International Journal of Man-Machine Studies* 7, 313-332

Maturana, Humberto R. 1978. *Biology of Language: The Epistemology of Reality*. In: Miller, George A./Lennberg, Elizabeth (Eds.). 1978. *Psychology and Biology of Language and Thought: Essays in Honor of Eric Lenneberg*, 27-63. New York: Academic Press

McKee, Robert. 1998 (1999). *Story. Substance, Structure, Style and the Principles of Screenwriting*. London: HarperCollins

Meltzoff, Andrew M./Decety, Jean. 2003. *What imitation tells us about social cognition: a rapprochement between developmental psychology and cognitive neuroscience*. In: Philosophical Transactions of The Royal Society, London B 358, 491-500

Meyer, Leonard B. 1956. *Emotion and Meaning in Music*. Chicago/London: University of Chicago Press

Mitchell, Robert W. 1994. *Multiplicities of self*. In: Parker, Sue Taylor/Mitchell, Robert W./Boccia, Maria L. (Eds.). 1994. *Self-awareness in animals and humans. Developmental perspectives*, 81-107. Cambridge: University Press

Morgan, Elaine. 1972. *Descent of Women*. London: Souvenir Press

Munz, Peter. 1993. *Philosophical Darwinism. On the origin of knowledge by means of natural selection*. London/New York: Routledge

Nussbaum, Martha C. 2010. *Not for Profit: Why Democracy Needs The Humanities*. Princeton, NJ: Princeton University Press

Öhman, Arne/Flyk, Anders/Lundqvist, Daniel. 2000. *Unconscious Emotion: Evolutionary Perspectives, Psychophysiological Data and Neuropsychological Mechanisms*. In: Lane, Richard D./Nadel, Lynn (Eds.). 2000. *Cognitive Neuroscience of Emotion*, 296-327. Oxford/New York: Oxford University Press

Olson, Randy. 2009. *Don't Be Such a Scientist: Talking Substance in an Age of Style*. Washington: Island Press

Padel, Ruth. 2007. *Introduction*. In: Forster, E.M. 1905 (2007). *Where Angels Fear To Tread*, ix-xix. London: Penguin

Panksepp, Jaak. 1994. *The Basics of Basic Emotion*. In: Ekman, Paul/Davidson, R.J. (Eds.). 1994. *The Nature of Emotion. Fundamental Questions*, 20-24. Oxford/New York: Oxford University Press

Panksepp, Jaak. 2003. *Feeling the pain of social loss*. In: Science 302, 237-239

Parker, Sue Taylor/Mitchell Robert W. 1994. *Self-awareness in Animals and Humans*. Cambridge: Cambridge University Press

Parker, Sue Taylor. 1998. *A Social Selection Model for the Evolution and Adaptive Significance of Self-Conscious Emotion*. In: Ferrari, Michel/Sternberg, Robert J. (Eds.). 1998. *Self Awareness. Its Nature and Development*, 108-136. New York: Guilford Press

Pascal, Blaise. ca. 1657 (1971). *Pensées et Opuscules*. Paris: Hachette

Paskow, Alan. 2004. *The Paradoxes of Art. A Phenomenological Investigation*. Cambridge: Cambridge University Press

Pitrou, Robert. 1950. *Musiker der Romantik*. Wien: Perneder. (Translation from French by Lolo Kraus and Dr. H. Halm, *Musiciens Romantiques*. 1946. Paris: Albin Michell)

Planalp, Sally. 1998. *Communicating Emotion in Everyday Life: Cues, Channels and Processes*. In: Andersen, Peter A./Guerrero, Laura K. (Eds.). 1998. *Handbook*

of Communication and Emotion. Research, Theory, Applications and Contexts, 29-47. San Diego: Academic Press
Plutchik, Robert. 1990. *Evolutionary bases of empathy.* In: Eisenberg, Nancy/Strayer, Janet (Eds.). 1990. *Empathy and its Development*, 38-46. Cambridge: Cambridge University Press
Popper, Karl R. 1956 (1996). *Realism and the Aim of Science.* London/New York: Routledge
Prainsack, Christoph. 2000. *Emotion and Generation of Meaning. An Essay in the Foundations of Experience.* Unpublished Master's thesis, University of Vienna
Prainsack, Christoph. 2004. *Is feeling thinking? A reassessment of the affect-cognition primacy debate from an information processing perspective.* Unpublished Ph. D. thesis, University of Vienna
Preziosi, Donald (Ed.). 1998. *The Art of Art History: A Critical Anthology.* Oxford/New York: Oxford University Press
Quine, Willard van Orman. 1960. *Word and Object.* Cambridge, MA: MIT Press
Quine, Willard van Orman. 1969. *Ontological Relativity and Other Essays.* New York/London: Columbia University Press
Read, Herbert. 1959 (1998). *A Concise History of Modern Painting.* London: Thames and Hudson
Redding, Paul. 1999. *The Logic of Affect.* Ithaca/London: Cornell University Press
Reich, Willi. 1959. *Frédéric Chopin, Briefe und Dokumente.* Zurich: Manesse
Rizzolatti, Giacomo/Fadiga, Luciano/Fogassi, Leonardo/Gallese, Vittorio. 2002. *From mirror neurons to imitation: facts and speculation.* In: Meltzoff, Andrew/Prinz, Wolfgang (Eds.). 2002. *The Imitative Mind*, 247-266. Cambridge: Cambridge University Press
Rizzolatti, Giacomo/Craighero, Laila/Fadiga, Luciano. 2003. *The mirror system in humans.* In: Stamenov, Maxim/Gallese Vittorio (Eds.). 2003. *Mirror Neurons and the Evolution of Brain and Language*, 37-59. Amsterdam: John Benjamins
Rizzolatti, Giacomo/Sinigaglia, Corrado. 2008. *Empathie und Spiegelneurone. Die biologische Basis des Mitgefühls.* Frankfurt am Main: Suhrkamp
Robinson, Douglas. 1991. *The Translator's Turn.* Baltimore: Hopkins University Press
Robinson, Douglas. 2003. *Performative Linguistics. Speaking and translating as doing things with words.* New York/London: Routledge
Robinson, Jenefer (Ed.). 1997. *Music and Meaning.* Ithaca/London: Cornell University Press
Robinson, Jenefer. 1997. *Introduction: New Ways of Thinking about Musical Meaning.* In: Robinson, Jenefer (Ed.). 1997. *Music and Meaning*, 1-20. Ithaca/London: Cornell University Press
Robinson, Marilynne. 2010. *Absence of Mind. The Dispelling of Inwardness from the Modern Myth of Self.* New Haven/London: Yale University Press
Rogers, Carl. 1975. *Empathic: An unappreciated way of being.* In: *The Counselling Psychologist* 2, 2-10
Rolls, Edmund T. 1999. *The Brain and Emotion.* Oxford/New York: Oxford University Press
Rothko, Mark. 2004. *The artist's reality.* New Haven/London: Yale University Press
Rousseau, Jean-Jacques. *Les rêveries du promeneur solitaire.* 1782 (1964). Paris: Garnier-Flammarion

Sadie, Stanley. 1980. *The New Grove Dictionary of Music and Musicians, vol.4*. London: Macmillan

Savage-Rumbaugh, Sue E. 1988. *Ape Language: From Conditioned Response to Symbol*. Oxford/New York: Oxford University Press

Schapiro, Meier. 1998. *The Still Life as a Personal Object – A Note on Heidegger and van Gogh*. In: Preziosi, Donald (Ed.). 1998. *The Art of Art History: A Critical Anthology*, 427-431. Oxford/New York: Oxford University Press

Scherer, Klaus R. 1994. *Evidence for Both Universality and Cultural Specificity of Emotion Elicitation*. In: Ekman, Paul/Davidson, R.J. (Eds.). 1994. *The Nature of Emotion. Fundamental Questions*, 172-175. Oxford/New York: Oxford University Press

Schrödinger, Erwin. 1922 (1997). *Was ist ein Naturgesetz? Beiträge zum naturwissenschafltichen Weltbild*. Munich: R. Oldenbourg

Schrödinger, Erwin. 1944 (2008). *What is life?* Cambridge: Cambridge University Press

Schrödinger, Erwin. 1951 (1996). *Science and Humanism*. Cambridge: Cambridge University Press

Schrödinger, Erwin. 1954 (1996). *Nature and the Greeks*. Cambridge: Cambridge University Press

Schrödinger, Erwin. 1958 (2008). *Mind and Matter*. Cambridge: Cambridge University Press

Schulz von Thun, Friedemann. 1981 (2001). *Miteinander Reden 1, Störungen und Klärungen. Allgemeine Psychologie der Kommuniaktion*. Reinbek bei Hamburg: Rowohlt

Segrin, Chris. 1998. *Interpersonal Communication Problems Associated with Depression and Loneliness*. In: Andersen, Peter A./Guerrero, Laura K. (Eds.). 1998. *Handbook of Communication and Emotion. Research, Theory, Applications and Contexts*, 215-242. San Diego: Academic Press

Snow, C. P. 1959 (1998). *The Two Cultures*. Cambridge: Cambridge University Press

Stern, Daniel. 1985. *The Interpersonal World of the Infant*. New York: Basic Books

Sternberg, Robert J./Spear-Swerling, Louise. 1998. *Personal Navigation*. In: Ferrari, Michel/Sternberg, Robert J. (Eds.). 1998. *Self Awareness. Its Nature and Development*, 219-245. New York: The Guilford Press

Strayer, Janet. 1990. *Affective and cognitive perspectives on empathy*. In: Eisenberg, Nancy/Strayer, Janet (Eds.). 1990. *Empathy and its Development*, 218-244. Cambridge: Cambridge University Press

Terada, Rei. 2001. *Feeling in Theory*. Harvard: Harvard University Press

Thompson, Ross A. 1990. *Empathy and emotional understanding: the early development of empathy*. In: Eisenberg, Nancy/Strayer, Janet (Eds.). 1990. *Empathy and its Development*, 119-145. Cambridge: Cambridge University Press

Thompson, William Forde. 2009. *Music, Thought, and Feeling. Understandig the Psychology of Music*. New York/Oxford: Oxford University Press

Treitler, Leo. 1997. *Language and the Interpretation of Music*. In: Robinson, Jenefer (Ed.). 1997. *Music and Meaning*, 23-56. Ithaca/London: Cornell University Press

Turner, Jonathan H. 2007. *Human Emotions*. London/New York: Routledge

Uexküll, Jakob von/Kriszat, Georg. 1970. *Streifzüge durch die Umwelten von Tieren und Menschen* (1934) und *Bedeutungslehre* (1940). Frankfurt am Main: Fischer
Vasari, Giorgio. 1550-1568 (1965, 1987). *Lives of the Artists*. Translation by George Bull. London: Penguin
Waal, Frans de. 2006 (2009). *Primates and Philosophers: How Morality Evolved*. Princeton: Princeton University Press
Wallner, Fritz. 1993. *Konstruktiver Realismus, Philosophie, Wissenschaft und Erziehung*. In: Fischer, Roland/Costazza, Markus/Pellert, Ada (Eds.). 1993. *Argumentation und Entscheidung. Zur Idee und Organisation von Wissenschaft*, 243-269. Munich/Vienna: Profil
Walton, Kendall. 1997. *Listening with Imagination: Is Music Representational?* In: Robinson, Jenefer (Ed.). 1997. *Music and Meaning*, 57-82. Ithaca/London: Cornell University Press
Watzlawick, Paul/Beavin Bavelas, Janet/Jackson, Don D. 1967. *Pragmatics of Human Communication. A Study of Interactional Patterns, Pathologies, and Paradoxes*. New York: W. W. Norton & Company
Wicker, Bruno/Keysers, Christian/Plailly, Jane/Royet, Jean-Pierre/Gallese, Vittorio/Rizzolatti, Giacomo. 2003. *Both of us are disgusted in my insula: the common neural basis of seeing and feeling disgust*. In: Neuron 40, 655-644
Wierzbicka, Anna. 1988. *The Semantics of Grammar*. Amsterdam/Philadelphia: John Benjamins
Williams, Simon J. 2001. *Emotion and social theory. Corporeal reflections on the (Ir)Rational*. London: Sage
Wispé, Lauren. 1990. *History of the concept of empathy*. In: Eisenberg, Nancy/Strayer, Janet (Eds.). 1990. *Empathy and its Development*, 17-37. Cambridge: Cambridge University Press
Wittgenstein, Ludwig. 1921 (1990). *Tractatus logico-philosophicus, Tagebücher 1914-1916; Philosophische Untersuchungen*. Frankfurt am Main: Suhrkamp
Zadro, Lisa/Arriaga, Ximena B./Williams, Kipling D. 2008. *Relational Ostracism*. In: Forgas, Joseph P./Fitness, Julie (Eds.). 2008. *Social Relationships. Cognitive, Affective, and Motivational Processes*, 305-320. New York: Psychology Press
Zajonc, Robert B. 1994. *Evidence for Nonconscious Emotions*. In: Ekman, Paul/Davidson, R.J. (Eds.). 1994. *The Nature of Emotion. Fundamental Questions*, 293-297. Oxford/New York: Oxford University Press

Index

A

Academia ... 9
Aesthetics ... 142
Affect ... 127, 149
Affective ... 126, 142, 144, 147, 150, 151
Age of Innocence ... 44, 87, 125, 139
Albom, Mitch ... 14, 113, 139
Alone ... 38, 39, 44, 45, 48, 72, 77, 86, 99, 114, 126, 131
Anna ... 13, 45, 119, 151
Anticipation ... 72
Aragon, Louis ... 41, 86, 140
Archer, Newland ... 44, 45, 87, 125
Archetype ... 68
Archimedes ... 85, 127
Aristotle ... 7, 57, 84, 114, 117, 121, 126, 139, 141, 145, 147
Arnheim, Rudolf ... 118, 129, 136, 141
Art ... 7, 85, 92, 94, 99, 115, 118, 121, 125, 127, 128, 30, 133, 139, 141, 143, 144, 146, 147, 148, 149, 150
Art of Rhetoric (Aristotle) ... 7, 117, 121, 139, 141, 147
Asparagus ... 23, 24, 25, 88, 139
Attachment ... 134
Auden, William ... 84, 140
Autopoiesis ... 129
Autopoietic systems ... 129

B

Babel, Tower of ... 23, 86, 98, 100
Backstory ... 80, 81, 94, 105
Back-up ... 56, 57, 62, 93, 98
Balmain, Pierre ... 19, 109
Bat baby ... 62, 63
Bath-night ... 15, 16, 47, 48, 88
Bear of Very Little Brain ... 61, 62
Beethoven, Ludwig van ... 31, 139
Being ... 74, 76, 120
Being-in-the-world ... 74
Benedict IX, Pope ... 53
Biocultural evolution ... 125, 143
Biological make-up ... 84
Bird ... 55, 56, 116, 118, 124, 146
Birtukaine ... 78, 111, 139
Black ... 68, 119
Blonde ... 68
Bouvard ... 107, 137, 139

153

Index

Box 70
Brittain, Vera 87, 129, 139
Broca's area 123, 145
Broken heart 86
Bruner, Jerome 117, 131, 136, 142
Butterfly, butterflies 27, 89

C

Cannon, Walter B. 125, 142
Categories 119, 122, 145, 146
Catharsis 113, 114, 115
Central glow 80, 122
Central theme 81
Chopin, Frédéric 39, 40, 41, 45, 65, 70, 88, 103, 114, 115, 139, 146, 149
Circle 53, 54, 55, 56, 57, 98, 99, 100, 101
Comics 120, 139, 143
Common experience 114
Communion 84, 92
Confusion 23, 47, 85, 100
Confusion of tongues 23
Content 124, 132
Continuity 118, 123
Cooper, Tommy 60, 61
Cortot, Alfred 40
Coup de foudre 107, 108, 137
Creative impulse 86
Cultural straitjacket 131

D

Damasio, Antonio 126, 133, 141, 143
Darling Ducks 71, 139
Darwin, Charles 126, 143
De Anima (Aristotle) 126, 139, 141
Denotation 122, 123, 132
Depression 150
Derrida, Jacques 115, 143
Descartes, René 97, 135, 139, 143
Dialect 56
Difference 61, 92, 103, 129, 133, 135
Disease 84
Dis-ease 83, 84, 99
Disorder 83, 84, 99, 118, 129, 141, 145
Dis-order 63, 83
Dissolution of unity 84
Distress 141
Ducks 71, 72, 139
Dvořák, Antonín 29, 73, 139

Index

E
E=mc² 57, 92, 94
Eddie 14, 15, 105, 108
Eeyore 61, 63
Eisner, Will 120, 139, 143
Ekman, Paul 133, 141, 142, 143, 144, 147, 148, 150, 151
Emotion 30, 80, 113, 114, 115, 122, 126, 132, 134,
141, 142, 143, 144, 146, 147, 148, 149, 150, 151
Emotional imperative 85, 94, 125
Emotional Intelligence 134, 145
Emotional pain 84
Emotional pulse 31
Emotionality 10
Empathy 127, 129, 130, 141, 143, 144, 149, 150, 151
Empty 72, 78, 81, 89, 121
Enemy 87
Enfer 114
Entropy 118, 141
Epistemology 148
Equations of meaning 94
Equivalence 128, 132, 135
Eureka 85, 127
Evidence 11, 23, 57, 73, 76, 84, 85, 93, 127, 134, 139, 141
Evidence proves 127
Evolution 125, 127, 143, 145, 146, 147, 148, 149
Evolutionary 97, 116, 122, 123, 125, 143, 144, 145, 149
Exactitude 44, 45, 55, 95, 101, 115, 135

F
Fact of life 94
Faith 127
Feelings 9, 13, 19, 24, 30, 35, 37, 39, 40, 44, 45, 47, 48,
56, 57, 61, 63, 72, 75, 79, 80, 81, 83, 84, 85, 91, 92,
97, 98, 105, 113, 124, 125, 127, 133, 134, 143, 149, 151
Fichte, Johann Gottlieb 121, 144
Fictional world 9, 120
Five people 14, 15, 105, 113, 139
Flaubert, Gustave 107, 108, 137, 139
Force of nature 91
Foreigner 48, 68
Forster, E. M. 80, 122, 139, 148
French 19, 20, 21, 30, 39, 109, 137
Frog 117

G
Galen of Pergamon 84, 126, 147
Gaskell, Elizabeth 79, 80, 139

Index

Germans 87
Gift of speech 29, 99
Giotto 53, 55, 56, 101
Goldman, David 67
Gould, Glenn 10
Goutte d'eau 39, 45
Grandmother 56, 116, 145
Grass is green 132
Grip 41
Gulda, Friedrich 10

H
Habermas, Jürgen 120, 145
Hale, Margaret 79
Happy ending 71, 105
Hard fact 91
Harmony 30, 83, 84, 99, 100, 129
Health 80, 84, 142
Heaven 13, 14, 15, 23, 38, 49, 105, 108, 109, 113, 139
Heidegger, Martin 74, 75, 76, 77, 78, 115, 120, 121, 139, 140, 144, 145, 150
Hell 15, 37, 38
Hepburn, Audrey 34, 88
Higgins, Nicholas 79, 80
Hitler, Adolf 56, 75, 116
Homeostasis 125, 142
Home-sick 84
Hug 83
Human urge 92
Humanities 9, 113
Hunch 80, 97
Husserl, Edmund 76

I
Imagination 30, 72, 85, 95, 120, 121, 125, 127
Imitation 114, 118, 123, 145, 148, 149
Indeterminacy 135
Inexpressible 81, 99
Infant 62
Inner life 81, 94
Inner meaning 81, 132
Inner need 86
Innocence 15, 55, 100
Inscrutable 135
Inspiration 85, 127
Interpersonal relations 144
Interpretation 10, 75, 77, 94, 114, 134
Irish 35, 65, 66, 88, 133

Index

Isolde ... 65, 70, 88

J
Jew ... 67, 68, 69, 119
Jigsaw ... 127, 128
Johnson, Dr. ... 57
Jude ... 69

K
Kaiser-Cooke, Michèle ... 128, 131, 136, 146
Kandinsky, Wassily ... 86, 128, 129, 139, 146
Kappus, Franz Xaver ... 81, 103
Keats, John ... 124, 140
Know what I mean ... 92, 94
Know what you mean ... 57, 94
Knowledge ... 80, 85, 105, 117, 121, 128, 136, 146, 148
Koestler, Arthur ... 127, 130, 146
Kress, Gunther ... 135, 146
Kripke, Saul ... 132, 146
Kuhn, Thomas ... 128, 146

L
Label ... 40, 45, 67, 70, 119
Lakoff, George ... 118, 119, 146
Language ... 9, 10, 23, 30, 57, 73, 77, 88, 92, 94, 99, 103, 116, 118, 119, 121, 122, 123, 124, 125, 127, 131, 132, 133, 140, 142, 143, 144, 145, 146, 148, 149, 150
Law of nature ... 91, 135
Light ... 25, 27, 41, 44, 45, 56, 74, 76, 77, 79, 80, 85, 88, 105, 108, 121
Light for the World ... 78, 111, 139
Lightning flash ... 107, 108
Liszt, Franz ... 65, 114
Literal ... 124, 125
Little Prince ... 55, 116
Living systems ... 88
Logic ... 77, 121, 125, 127, 131, 132, 133, 149
Logical equivalence ... 128
Loneliness ... 142, 150
Longing ... 99
Love ... 7, 13, 14, 29, 30, 43, 44, 65, 67, 70, 71, 72, 73, 78, 79, 80, 84, 87, 103, 105, 107, 108, 119, 130, 133, 136
Love-sick ... 84
Love-story ... 108
Luhmann, Niklas ... 117, 126, 147

M
Ma Solitude ... 38, 111, 139

157

Index

Manet, Edouard	23, 24, 25, 88, 139
Mary	65, 66, 67, 70, 88, 103, 142, 146
Mathematical logic	131, 132
Matisse, Henri	44, 115, 139, 141
Maturana, Humberto	88, 119, 123, 124, 125, 126, 129, 147, 148
Meaning	44, 65, 76, 80, 85, 117, 119, 120, 124, 128, 129, 132, 136, 142
Meaning in Music	148
Memory	15, 72, 134
Mess	63
Metaphor	117, 118, 144, 146
Mind	19, 21, 53, 118
Mirror neurons	123, 149
Misunderstand	119
Morgan, Elaine	116, 148
Mot juste	108
Mother-infant	118, 143, 144
Moustaki, Georges	38, 111, 139
Mozart, Wolfgang Amadeus	10
Mum	16, 34, 88
Music	17, 19, 29, 30, 31, 39, 45, 51, 70, 73, 79, 81, 92, 99, 113, 114, 120, 125, 130, 143, 145
Mutual recognition	108
My heart leaps up	36

N

Name	13, 19, 20, 23, 36, 39, 40, 65, 66, 67, 68, 70, 88, 107, 109, 114
Naming	40, 65, 68, 88, 119
National Socialist	75, 76, 78
Nationalsozialismus	144, 145
Natural sciences	135
Natural selection	148
Nature	25, 35, 36, 37, 134, 135, 142, 143, 144, 145, 146, 147, 148, 150, 151
Nazi	74, 76
Nerd	56
Neural pathways	126
Neutral vantage point	130
Nigger	119
Ninth Symphony	31
Non-scientist	9, 127
North and South	79, 139
Not communicate	135
Not-understand	94, 95, 97, 98, 100, 108

Index

O
Objective relativity ... 131
Ode to Joy ... 31
Opera ... 29, 30, 114
Order ... 55, 62, 63, 67, 73, 76, 78, 79, 80, 83, 85, 98, 99, 105, 117, 118, 124, 130, 136

P
Pain ... 14, 45, 47, 84, 85, 86, 88, 99, 125, 126, 142, 147, 148
Painter ... 9, 139
Pair of shoes ... 43, 44, 139
Pars pro toto ... 44, 45
Pascal, Blaise ... 77, 97, 121, 136, 140, 148
Passion ... 23, 29, 31, 44, 73, 79, 85, 86, 107, 108, 137
Pattern ... 15, 45, 98
Pécuchet ... 107, 137, 139
Perception ... 119, 127, 128, 131, 147
Perspectival listening ... 130, 145
Perspectival shift ... 130
Perspective ... 123, 130, 131, 136, 149
Perturbation ... 129, 133, 135
Physical pain ... 84, 126
Piglet ... 61, 62
Poet ... 9, 103, 121, 129, 137
Poetics (Aristotle) ... 114, 117, 139, 141, 145
Pooh Bear ... 61, 62, 63, 139
Pope, Benedict IX ... 53, 54, 55, 56
Popper, Karl ... 128, 149
Precision ... 55, 135
Primate ... 122, 123, 145, 151
Private language ... 131, 146
Proof ... 53, 92, 93
Psyche ... 84, 126
Psychobiology ... 142

Q
Quine, Willard van Orman ... 135, 149

R
Rainbow ... 35, 36, 130
Raindrop ... 39, 40, 41, 45, 65, 70, 114
Rational ... 85, 97, 151
Reality ... 9, 57, 84, 85, 86, 88, 89, 92, 113, 119, 128, 132, 133, 134, 135, 136, 139, 146, 148, 149
Reason ... 77, 97, 121, 136, 142
Recognition ... 33, 62, 75, 85, 105, 108, 117, 123, 145
Reference ... 135

Index

Regentropfen 39, 45
Rejection 126, 143
Relational Ostracism 151
Relationship 124, 143, 147
Relativism 131
Re-scramble 63, 105
Rhetoric, Art of (Aristotle) 7, 117, 121, 139, 141, 147
Rhythm 10, 30, 31
Rilke, Rainer Maria 81, 103, 119, 140
Rogers, Carl 130, 149
Roosevelt, Eleanor 60, 61
Rothko, Mark 115, 121, 133, 139, 149
Rousseau, Jean-Jacques 133, 140, 149
Rusalka 29, 31, 73, 139

S

Sad music 113
Saint-Exupéry, Antoine de 55, 116, 139
Same difference 103
Same enough 45, 48
Sand, George 114, 139
Sartre, Jean-Paul 35, 37, 114, 139
Schapiro, Meier 115, 150
Schrödinger, Erwin 113, 118, 134, 135, 150
Science 9, 84, 85, 92, 94, 98, 99, 113, 116, 117,
                                            125, 127, 128, 130, 136, 143, 144, 146, 148, 149, 150
Scientific evidence 93
Scientist 9, 56, 97, 125, 148
Sci-speak 9
Sci-vision 9
Screenplay 80, 121
Sein und Zeit 74, 120, 139, 145
Self-awareness 144, 145, 148
Shared manifold hypothesis 144
Sharing 84, 92, 115, 124
Sharing values 115
Shenonnypa 20, 73
Shoes 43, 44, 45, 115
Silence 21, 29, 30, 31, 41, 70, 72, 73, 78, 81, 94, 120, 125
Sillitoe, Alan 127, 128, 139
Sin 10
Social attachment 126, 145
Social cognition 141, 148
Social exclusion 126, 143, 147
Social interaction 123, 134, 141
Social isolation 126
Social loss 126, 148

Index

Softies 84
Solutio continuitatis 84
Soma 84, 126
Somatic knowledge 121
Soul 41, 84, 85, 86, 124, 126, 139, 141
Soul knowledge 85
Space 39, 70, 72, 73, 74, 75, 76, 77, 78, 79, 80,
81, 85, 88, 89, 94, 95, 99, 120, 121, 129, 130
Stone 57, 63, 76, 91, 92
Stoned 91, 134, 139
Subjectivity 10
Surprise 60, 117, 131
Systems 83, 88, 119, 123, 124, 125, 126, 129, 131, 132, 141

T
Tea-bag 59, 60, 63
Tea-bag principle 63
Theory of mind 123, 127, 145
Thing 61, 62, 63, 98
Thornton, John 79, 80
Tightrope 100
Time 74, 120
Tourist 35, 36, 140
Tower of Babel 23, 86, 98, 100
Translation 10, 31, 116, 119, 120, 128, 135, 139, 144, 145, 146
Translator 16, 97, 136
truth 9, 10, 23, 39, 44, 45, 54, 56, 57, 74, 81, 86, 92, 93,
94, 95, 98, 101, 105, 108, 115, 116, 124,
125, 127, 129, 132, 133, 134
Truth 76, 77, 121, 133, 140, 143, 145
Tummy-ache 13, 16, 45
Typical 66, 68

U
Uncertainty 94, 95, 100, 135
Universal 67, 68, 87, 99, 133
Un-recognise 75
Un-think 76

V
van Gogh, Vincent 43, 44, 45, 115, 139, 150
Vasari, Giorgio 53, 54, 116, 151
Verification 127
Vérité 44, 115, 133
Voice of the soul 86

W

Waal, Frans de	123, 151
Water-spirit	29, 73
Watzlawick, Paul	135, 151
Wharton, Edith	44, 87, 125, 139
What-we-can-be	74
Wittgenstein, Ludwig	131, 132, 146, 151
Wodge	47
Wordsworth, William	35, 36, 37, 115, 140

Translation Happens

Edited by Michèle Cooke

Vol. 1   Michèle Cooke: The Lightning Flash. Language, longing and the facts of life. 2011.

www.peterlang.de

Barbara Lewandowska-Tomaszczyk / Marcel Thelen (eds.)

Meaning in Translation

Frankfurt am Main, Berlin, Bern, Bruxelles, New York, Oxford, Wien, 2010.
480 pp., num. fig. and tab.
Łodź Studies in Language. Edited by Barbara Lewandowska-Tomaszczyk.
Vol. 19
ISBN 978-3-631-60105-1 · hardback € 79,80*

«This anthology edited by Barbara Lewandowska-Tomaszczyk and Marcel Thelen will be of considerable interest to all Translation Studies students and academics. It demonstrates the energy and intellectual commitment that these two researchers have devoted to Translation Studies in the last twenty years. Their book series *Translation and Meaning* from which this anthology was mainly composed and the 5-yearly Maastricht--Łódź Duo Colloquia of the same name that they have been organising since 1990 have become internationally well-known for their breath of topics and up-to-date themes. Articles spanning two decades give a unique historical perspective to the volume, highlighting seminal moments of the development of what is now established as an interdisciplinary and international field. Renowned scholars such as Eugene Nida, Peter Newmark, Albrecht Neubert, Christiane Nord, Gideon Toury, Mona Baker, Anthony Pym, Mary Snell-Hornby and Ernst-August Gutt are writing alongside new scholarly voices in diverse investigations of meaning in translation-related areas. The book is of outstanding quality and should be in every Translation Studies library.»
Lucile Desblache, Reader in Translation, Roehampton University
Editor of *JoSTrans*, The Journal of Specialised Translation

Content: Lexicology · Terminology · Cognitive Linguistics · Corpora · Culture · Skopos-oriented Translation · Indeterminacy · Lexical Semantics · Prototypical Definition of Translation · Translation Problem · Semantic Net · Relevance · Translation of Secondary Functions · Bible Translation · Metaphors in Life Scences · Figurative Language · Audiovisual Translation · Translator Training

Frankfurt am Main · Berlin · Bern · Bruxelles · New York · Oxford · Wien
Distribution: Verlag Peter Lang AG
Moosstr. 1, CH-2542 Pieterlen
Telefax 0041 (0)32/376 17 27

*The €-price includes German tax rate
Prices are subject to change without notice
Homepage http://www.peterlang.de